BOOK E
READING FOR CONCEPTS

"All things are changed, and we change with them." Lothair I

WILLIAM LIDDLE

General Editor
Director, Instructional Services
Colorado Springs Public Schools
Director of the Reading Clinic, the Colorado College
Colorado Springs, Colorado

BOOK E
READING

FOR CONCEPTS
Second Edition

WEBSTER DIVISION
McGRAW-HILL BOOK COMPANY

New York   St. Louis   San Francisco
Aukland   Bogotá   Düsseldorf   Johannesburg   London   Madrid
Mexico   Montreal   New Delhi   Panama   Paris   São Paulo
Singapore   Sydney   Tokyo   Toronto

Contributing Authors for the Reading for Concepts Series:

Linda Barton, feature writer for *St. Louis Today.*

Roberta H. Berry, elementary school teacher, writer.

Barbara Broeking, journalist and educational publications editor.

Eth Clifford, author of many volumes of fiction and poetry for youth.

Ellen Dolan, juvenile book author.

Barbara R. Frey, Professor of Education, State University College, Buffalo, N.Y.

Ruth Harley, author and editor of young people's periodicals.

Phyllis W. Kirk, children's book editor.

Richard Kirk, author of science, social studies, and reading books for youth.

Thomas D. Mantel, attorney and juvenile author.

Marilyn F. Peachin, journalist and editor.

James N. Rogers, author-editor of science and social studies resource books.

James J. Pflaum, author and editor of current events periodicals.

Gloria S. Rosenzweig, writer of primary teaching materials.

Jean Shirley, author of juvenile books.

Rosemary Winebrenner, editor of children's books.

Jean White, journalist and writer of young people's reference materials.

Educational Consultant:

Dr. Ruth Gallant, The Center for Teaching and Learning, University of North Dakota, Grand Forks, N.D.

Statisticians for Original Prepublication Field Trials:

Dr. Michael Grady and Dr. Roslyn Grady, Colorado Springs, Colo.

Robert Hampson, Pupil Accounting and Testing Services, Colorado Springs, Colo.

Resource Committee:

Ruth Liddle, Eleanor Wier, Ruth Mitchell, Jean Keeley, and Joseph Tockman.

Project Editor: Carol Washburne
Designer: Jim Darby
Editing Supervisor: Sal Allocco
Production Supervisor: Karen Romano

Illustrators: James Cummings; Portia Takajian, GAI
Cover Photo: René Burri/Magnum

ISBN 0-07-037665-4

TABLE OF CONTENTS

Concept III: *The Success of a Community Depends on Cooperation Among Its Members*

Purpose

This book is one of eight in the series "Reading for Concepts." It was designed to provide an opportunity for young readers to grow in reading experience while exploring a wide variety of ideas contained in several of the academic disciplines.

Three basic underlying concepts are reflected in this book. They are: *Nature or humans limit things that can be done; The use of earth, space, and materials depends on the needs of the users;* and *The success of a community depends on cooperation among its members.*

To illustrate these concepts, stories have been written around intriguing pieces of information which reflect these ideas. The content has been drawn from the nine disciplines of space, history, biology, economics, anthropology, geography, earth science, political science, and art. In this way a wide array of content for meeting various interests has been assured.

Two or three stories are presented in each discipline. A narrative follows after stories 18, 45, and 72. The narratives, largely drawn from folk literature, will provide a change of pace and are "just for fun" types of stories.

Teaching Procedure

The child will be given a diagnostic test at the beginning of the program to help the teacher in determining at which reading level he or she should be placed.

1. Discuss the title and picture clue in the story and establish purposes for reading it.

2. Present difficult words in advance. (There is an index at the back of this book which will direct the teacher in selecting the words expected to cause difficulties at each reading level.)

3. Have students read the story silently. A timed approach may be useful. The stories are all approximately 220 words long. Narratives lengths are listed. Begin with a reading time suitable to the average needs of the group. Moderate speed in reading is an indication of reading proficiency, but it is not the basic province of this series. As comprehension increases, the emphasis may switch to reducing reading time. At this time, use a stopwatch and figure each reader's rate for a story and encourage the pupil to read more quickly each subsequent time. By using the charts, pupils can see their own progress.

4. Following each regular story is a test which is especially designed to improve specific skills in reading. There are charts at the end of this book on which to record scores of each skill tested. By carefully using these charts, teacher and pupil can make a diagnosis of specific skill weaknesses and also keep track of progress in each aspect of reading skill.

The sample exercise that begins the pupil's text should be reviewed carefully with all pupils. Each test item in the sample should be examined. Pupils should understand in advance exactly how they are to arrive at correct answers, whether they are expected to retain information, to verify from the text, to find the exact word needed, or to conjecture on the basis of information given. Success is necessary. The sample exercise will be found at the end of this discussion.

The skills tested in Book E are typical of those suggested in Bloom's *Taxonomy of Educational Objectives*. Bloom's Taxonomy is a way of ordering thinking from recall, the simplest thought process, to the most abstract order of thinking, synthesis. A taxonomy is a scale, the use of which is a means of establishing where along a hierarchy of thinking one is operating. The point of the test questions is to build a series of test items that incorporate the range of thinking skills as they are reflected in the Taxonomy.

Item 1. Knowledge of specific facts. The answers here must be selected from a group of possibilities. The correct answer selected from multiple alternatives is a directly stated fact in the story. This retention skill would correspond to Bloom's knowledge category, especially to "Knowledge of Specific Facts." The nature of the articles, of course, contributes to the awareness of some key facts about particular cultures, etc.

Item 2. Recognition of meaning of word in context. The student must choose and write the correct response. This skill corresponds to Bloom's "Knowledge of Terminology," especially to the area of "Familiarity with a large number of words in their common range of meaning."

Item 3. This item is intended to make pupils aware of correct form and usage. The student must select the word, or words, described by the words used in the stem of the question. It may be an adjective, a descriptive phrase, or even the predicate of the sentence. The student must find the necessary word in the story and write it. This skill falls within Bloom's "Knowledge of Conventions."

Item 4. Recognition of implications or inferences. This item requires selecting the correct inference from several choices. The response required comes from a multiple choice of implied details. The skill relates to Bloom's "Extrapolation."

Item 5. Knowledge of specific facts. The answers here must be selected from a group of possibilities. The correct answer selected from multiple alternatives is a directly stated fact in the story. This retention skill would correspond to Bloom's knowledge category, especially to "Knowledge of Specific Facts." The nature of the articles, of course, contributes to the awareness of some key facts about particular cultures, etc.

Item 6. Ability to make substantiation from content. This item requires the reader to reread to prove a point. The reader must determine whether or not the given statement is in the story. This skill is specifically one of attention to the task of reading.

Item 7. Recognition of the meaning of the whole. This item requires the reader to select the answer which best describes the central theme of the story. This skill corresponds to Bloom's "Meaning of the Whole — Interpretation."

Item 8. This item expects the learner to make an interpretation. The reader must confirm an understanding of the nature of a fact, process, or problem. He or she must select the one response among the given alternatives which most nearly shows the cause, or the meaning, of the stated effect as explained in the story. This item corresponds to Bloom's level two of thinking: "Comprehension."

Item 9. Recognition of implications or

inferences. This item requires selecting the correct inference from several choices. The response required comes from a multiple choice of implied details. The skill relates to Bloom's "Extrapolation."

Method

Each story has been written to the specifications for a controlled vocabulary and readability level. The readability level of this book was determined through application of the Dale-Chall Readability Formula. See the manual for statistical information.

Words not in the controlled vocabulary list were limited to words according to standard lists of words suitable for pupils slightly older than their reading level would imply. In some cases, the content required the use of a highly specialized word. Such words are carefully defined by context clues in the story itself and are listed in the index.

Field Testing

In the testing population, a wide range of background and abilities of pupils were represented. See the manual for details. The results of extensive field testing were used to revise the materials until an optimum ease index was achieved. Preliminary practice should be provided. See teaching notes for the practice selection for specific directions necessary to make each question a learning experience.

The teacher should also remind the reader where it is necessary to look back into the story to find answers.

Concept Recapitulations

After pupils have completed the text, the following suggestions may be helpful in conducting a discussion which will tie together the information carried in the individual articles in terms of the overall concept. This type of activity is important not for the particular information pupils will meet in these books but for the beginnings of building a wider view of the human environment. Information from widely divergent fields can interact to contribute to broad, intellectual awareness, whereas most education tends to fracture rather than serve the development of such wide-angle perspective.

Often, those youngsters most resistant to formal educational processing have drawn their own conclusions about the world and how it works. These students, in particular, may take fresh challenge from the experience of using pieces of information as the flexible building blocks for at least one unified meaningful whole. This type of reading is helping them practice the necessary modern skill of "continuous translation." Here skill building in reading has been attached not only to immediate short-range motivation and information accumulation but also to long-range creative reassessment of apparently dissimilar content. Great openness and considerable flexibility will be required from teachers who will make the greatest use of this aspect of this reading program. The possibilities for student growth and awakenings are enormous.

A procedure such as the following is suggested:

"You have read stories about three big ideas. The first idea was that *nature or humans limit things that can be done.* In the beginning of the book you were asked to keep certain questions in mind. Can you answer these questions now?" (Pupils meet guiding questions on page 13.)

1. Can you think of something that is impossible to do now?

2. Will it ever be possible to do this?

3. What change might occur if this thing were possible?

4. Why hasn't somebody done this thing already?

5. Do you think you might be able to find a way to achieve this?

"The second big idea that you read about was that *the use of earth, space, and materials depends on the needs of the users.* Can you now answer the following questions?" (Guide questions are on page 53.)

1. What things do you need?

2. Do all people need the same things you do?

3. What causes other people's needs to be different than yours?

4. Does it take the same materials to meet the needs of all people?

5. Do we use up all the materials that are available to us?

"The third big idea that you read about was that *the success of a community depends on cooperation among its members.* Can you answer these questions now?" (Guide questions are on page 111.)

1. What are five things that help to make a good community?

2. How can you help to make a better community?

3. What are some things that you could have by living in a community that you could not have if you lived alone?

4. Can anyone help make a better community?

5. Can you think of some ways that people cooperate in a community?

Have a few priming possibilities ready to suggest, or shape them out of the early offerings from the group. Sophisticated statements and a review of specifics are not to be expected. Look for signs of mental play and the movement of information from one setting to another. It is perfectly reasonable to conclude with unanswered questions for pupils to ponder in retrospect. However, it is important to give pupils the satisfaction of enthusiastic acceptance of their early attempts at this type of open-ended speculation.

STEPS FOR THE READER

A. Turn to page 14. Look at the picture. Read the title. Think about what the story will say.

B. Study the words for this page on the list beginning page 172.

C. Read the story carefully.

D. Put your name and the title of the story on a sheet of paper. Number from one to nine. Begin the test on the page next to the story.

1. This question asks you to remember something the story has told you. Which of the four choices is correct for this sentence?

2. This question asks you to find the word in the story that means the same as the words in italics. The question gives you a paragraph number. Read that part again to be sure you have the right word.

3. Reread the paragraph given. Which word or words are described by the words given in the question? The given words must modify or explain the noun you select.

4. This question wants you to think about the story. The answer is not in your book. Read the choices. Choose the one that is the very best guess you might make from the ideas you have just read.

5. The question tests your memory for a detail. Which of the choices agrees with the story?

6. The question requires that you confirm whether or not an idea was actually presented in the story you have just read. If the sentence is wrong according to the information you have just read, choose *No*. If the information was not given at all, be sure to answer *Does not say*.

7. This question asks you to choose a statement about the entire story. Don't select an idea that fits only one small part. Your answer should fit all of the story.

8. The story gives you the information you need. Refer to it again to be sure which of the given choices is the best explanation.

9. On the basis of the story, which of the choices is most likely to be true? The answer is not in the story. You will have to think about the ideas and draw your own conclusions.

E. Check your work. The answers for the first test are given below. Your teacher may let you use the answer key for other tests. She or he may check your work for you.

F. Put the number correct at the top of your paper. Now go back and recheck the answers that were wrong. Do you see now how the correct answer was better? How can you get ready to do the next test better?

G. Turn to page 170. The directions tell you how to put your score onto a record chart. Your teacher will tell you if you may write in the book, or how to make a copy.

Looking for the Big Idea
Your stories are grouped together to point to big ideas called concepts. Before each new concept group, there is an opening page to direct your reading for these overview ideas.

Just For Fun
Your book has three longer stories that are just for fun. These stories, beginning on pages 50, 108, and 166, are from old folktales. There are no questions to answer.

Answers for Practice Test, page 15

1. c	2. object	3. Alpha Centauri
4. b	5. c	6. No
7. a	8. b	9. c

I

Nature Or Humans Limit Things That Can Be Done

In this section you will read about how nature or humans limit things that can be done. You will read about these things from the standpoint of space, history, biology, economics, anthropology, geography, earth science, political science, and art.

Keep these questions in mind when you are reading.

1. What are some things that seem impossible to do now?

2. Do you think any of these things will ever be done?

3. How might it affect you if these things were possible?

4. What is preventing these goals from being reached?

5. From your knowledge of the past, do you feel some of these things will happen soon?

Nothing Can Move That Fast

In many stories on TV and in science-fiction books, humans travel to faraway stars. They have quick, easy journeys. But so far, people have been able to reach only the earth's own moon.

Suppose a person wanted to reach a faraway star. It would take a lifetime of travel for someone to move faster than the speed of light. Nothing can move that fast except light itself.

Strange things happen to an object when it moves rapidly. The object weighs more. An object moving at 86 percent of the speed of light is twice as heavy as it is at rest. A stick appears shorter. A clock runs more slowly. A person would not age so fast in space as on the earth.

Light travels more than 186,000 miles a second, or about 11 million miles a minute. In one year, light travels 6 trillion (6,000,000,000,000) miles. That great distance is called a light-year. It is used to measure distances in space.

The star closest to our sun is Alpha Centauri (al′fə sen tôr′ē). It is more than four light-years away. A human traveling at the speed of light could make a round trip to Alpha Centauri in nine years. But even at that speed, this person could not reach Alcaid (al kād′) in the handle of the Big Dipper. A one-way journey to Alcaid would take almost 200 years!

FIND THE ANSWERS

1. The star closest to our sun is
   - a. Alcaid.
   - b. the Big Dipper.
   - c. Alpha Centauri.
   - d. Rigel.

2. The word in paragraph 3 that means *a thing* or *something* is

   _____.

3. The words "closest to our sun" in the last paragraph describe the star

   _____ _____.

4. The story does not say so, but it makes you think that
   - a. humans will soon make a one-way trip to Alcaid.
   - b. it would take over four years to go to Alpha Centauri.
   - c. the handle of the Big Dipper is not many light-years away.

5. A one-way journey to Alcaid would take
   - a. about nine years.
   - b. less than four years.
   - c. almost 200 years.

6. When things move rapidly, they stay the same as they are when motionless.

   Yes   No   Does not say

7. On the whole, this story is about
   - a. the problems of traveling to faraway stars.
   - b. the distance between our sun and the other stars.
   - c. what happens when we travel faster than the speed of light.

8. Why do we measure great distances in light-years instead of miles?
   - a. Units of light-years sound better.
   - b. Using light-years reduces the number of figures used.
   - c. We used to measure distances in light-years long ago.

9. Which statement does the story lead you to believe?
   - a. Light travels several hundred miles in a year.
   - b. It is not possible for humans to get to the nearest star.
   - c. Going to the moon is easier than reaching Alcaid.

New Tools for an Old Science

Astronomy is the oldest science known to humans. Thousands of years ago people looked at the stars in wonder. But they were limited by what they could see with their eyes alone.

The Greeks studied astronomy over 2,000 years ago. They saw the size, color, and brightness of stars. They watched the stars move as the seasons changed. But the Greeks had no tools to help them study the heavens.

Until telescopes were invented, people knew little about the moon. They did not know that the planet called Saturn had rings around it. They could not see all the planets.

Each new tool helped people to study the heavens. In the 1700s a German named William Herschel improved telescopes in England. He was helped greatly by his sister Caroline who gave up a promising life in music to study astronomy with him. In 1786 she made important findings herself. Caroline Herschel discovered eight comets in eleven years.

Pluto was first seen in 1930. It was the last of nine planets to be discovered. More recently scientists used the spectroscope to learn what gases made up our sun. Radio telescopes now confirm waves reaching us from far out in space.

Today, astronomy is a fast growing science. We have learned more in the last fifty years than in the whole history of astronomy.

1. Caroline Herschel discovered
   a. noises in space.
   b. eight comets.
   c. about fifty planets.
   d. no planets.

2. The word in the first paragraph that means *not able to go beyond* is

   _____ .

3. The words "the oldest science known to humans" in the first paragraph

   describe _____ .

4. The story does not say so, but it makes you think that
   a. people's eyes have grown weaker in the last fifty years.
   b. Caroline Herschel devoted her life to astronomy.
   c. stars far out in space do not have color.

5. The last planet to be discovered was
   a. Saturn.
   b. Mars.
   c. Pluto.

6. Saturn has rings around it.
   Yes   No   Does not say

7. On the whole, this story is about
   a. the way Caroline Herschel played the piano.
   b. discoveries in astronomy.
   c. the six planets as we now know them.

8. Why didn't people know about Pluto until 1930?
   a. Their telescopes weren't strong enough to see it.
   b. Pluto didn't come into being until 1930.
   c. Space was too dark to see any of the planets.

9. Which statement does the story lead you to believe?
   a. Telescopes were discovered by the Greeks 2,000 years ago.
   b. More discoveries in astronomy may be made.
   c. All the stars can be seen with the eyes alone.

One-Eyed People and Terrible Monsters

In 1492, Columbus sailed the Atlantic Ocean. Up to that time, sailors from central Europe did not dare to head west across the sea. Many dangers held them back. Their maps showed the unexplored parts of the world as dangerous and frightening.

In those days, mapmakers did not know what the world was really like. They used their imagination. They showed the earth as a large circle with Europe and Asia in the center. Around the edges of the circle, they showed swamps, deserts, and the ocean. A race of one-eyed people and terrible monsters were supposed to live there.

The ocean itself was called the Sea of Darkness. Sailors believed that if they sailed far north they would reach mountains made of ice. They thought that far south the ocean turned into fire and boiling water. They were afraid to sail east or west. They thought they would fall off the earth.

A sailor had to face some dangers that were quite real. At that time, ships were not made with metal as they are today. Shipworms could attack a boat's wooden planking. A sailing vessel might look sound but

be eaten through. It might go to pieces at sea and sink.

1. Early mapmakers showed the center of the earth as
   a. the Sea of Darkness.   c. Europe and Asia.
   b. swamps and deserts.   d. icy mountains.

2. The word in the first paragraph that means *not known* is

   _____.

3. The words "a large circle" in paragraph 2 refer to the

   _____.

4. The story does not say so, but it makes you think that
   a. sailors thought the world was flat.
   b. mapmakers had seen one-eyed monsters.
   c. early sailing vessels were made of metal.

5. A real danger that sailors faced was
   a. seas of boiling water.
   b. terrible monsters.
   c. wooden ships filled with shipworms.

6. Columbus sailed in the Pacific Ocean.
   Yes   No   Does not say

7. On the whole, this story is about
   a. how to draw a map of Europe and Asia.
   b. the real and unreal dangers of early sailing.
   c. the lands where one-eyed people lived.

8. Why did the mapmakers have to use their imaginations?
   a. Each person wanted to have a different map.
   b. They did not like to draw the world as it really was.
   c. No one knew what the world was really like.

9. Which statement does the story lead you to believe?
   a. Fear keeps people from doing new things.
   b. Early sailors could not read maps.
   c. The oceans of the world were once dark.

They Were Not Free

In Europe during the Middle Ages, landowners were called nobles. They lived in large castles with their families. They had many people to protect them. The nobles spent most of their time fighting, hunting, and eating. They owned hundreds of acres of land.

On this land lived peasants called serfs. Serfs were not free people. A serf could use land belonging to the noble and could raise crops to eat. But in return the serf had to work for the noble without pay.

A serf had to spend at least three days a week farming land. Each spring, the land of the nobles had to be plowed by serfs. Only then could serfs plow land for their own crops. Serfs also had to give the nobles some of their own grain after harvest time.

A serf owned nothing. The forests belonged to the nobles, and serfs could not hunt there. A serf could use a noble's mill to grind the grain, but some grain had to be left for the noble. The serfs baked bread in ovens belonging to the nobles. Each time they had to leave a loaf of bread for the noble.

A serf belonged to the noble, just as the land did. Serfs had to obey the nobles. They could not leave the land without permission.

1. Landowners were called
   a. fighters.   b. nobles.   c. eaters.

2. A serf owned
   a. some land.   c. a plow.
   b. nothing.   d. the forest.

3. The words "They lived in large castles with their families" in paragraph 1 describe _____.

4. The story does not say so, but it makes you think that
   a. a serf did not have an easy life.
   b. serfs usually became nobles.
   c. a serf spent free time hunting.

5. A serf spent much time
   a. in the house resting.
   b. fighting, hunting, and eating.
   c. farming land for the noble.

6. A serf could leave the land whenever the noble agreed.
   Yes   No   Does not say

7. On the whole, this story is about
   a. a worker's life during the Middle Ages.
   b. how bread was made from ground grain.
   c. life in a large castle during the last century.

8. Why did serfs work for nobles without pay?
   a. They liked that kind of life better than any other.
   b. To have the use of some of the land to raise their own crops.
   c. Each serf wanted to be invited to the noble's castle.

9. Which statement does the story lead you to believe?
   a. Serfs had a lot of freedom.
   b. Serfs fought for the nobles.
   c. Serfs were very poor.

Old and New Enemies

One hundred years ago, sea otters lived on islands off Alaska. They spent their lives on land as well as in the ocean. On land, they found food, slept, and had their young. In the ocean, they swam, splashed, and played.

Then Russians came to the islands and hunted sea otters for their fur. They were paid over $500 for each otter skin. Thousands of these animals were killed by the Russians.

In 1867, the United States bought Alaska, and the Americans began to hunt sea otters. So many animals were killed that few were left. At last, in 1916, our country passed a law that sea otters could not be killed.

By then, the remaining animals had left their island homes. To escape humans, they had moved to beds of seaweed far from the shore.

Now the ocean is the sea otter's only home. The otters live in the giant seaweed and feed on sea urchins, clams, and crabs. To sleep, they wrap themselves and their young in long strands of seaweed. Because the babies must be taught to swim and dive, they float on their backs until they learn to swim well.

In the sea the otters now face a new enemy. Hidden by seaweed, they watch for killer whales. Because of their old enemies, humans, they can no longer live on land.

1. The sea otters' new enemies are
   a. humans.
   b. killer whales.
   c. sea urchins.
   d. strands of seaweed.

2. The word in paragraph 5 that means *small sea animals* is sea

   _____.

3. The words "the sea otter's only home" in paragraph 5 refer to the

   _____.

4. The story does not say so, but it makes you think that
   a. sea otters are very smart.
   b. there are no sea otters alive today.
   c. sea otters cannot sleep in the sea.

5. Sea otters now spend their whole lives
   a. on the land.
   b. in the ocean.
   c. wrapped in seaweed.

6. Sea otter babies must be taught to swim.
   Yes   No   Does not say

7. On the whole, this story is about
   a. the American hunters who killed thousands of animals.
   b. the islands off the coast of Alaska.
   c. how sea otters have changed their way of life.

8. Why did sea otters leave the land?
   a. They had to escape from humans.
   b. They learned to swim in the ocean.
   c. They joined their friends, the killer whales.

9. Which statement does the story lead you to believe?
   a. America passed a law about killer whales.
   b. Sea otters once spent as much time on land as in the sea.
   c. Sea otters look like fish because they have smooth skins.

Too Many Lemmings

In the mountains of Scandinavia (skan′də nā′vē ə) live small rodents called lemmings. Lemmings live together in colonies and feed on moss, roots, leaves, and bark.

Because lemmings have many young, the population of a colony grows rapidly. There comes a time when the colony becomes so crowded that the animals cannot find enough food. Then some lemmings must leave.

The lemmings move down from the mountains into the valleys. For a short while, they can find enough food. But their population again becomes too large. They march on, eating everything growing in their path.

On their journey, the lemmings climb mountains and swim lakes and streams. Some die from disease. Some drown in rivers, and some are killed by hawks and other animals. Many die from becoming too tired. After so many die, the remaining lemmings have enough food. But in three to twenty years, some must once again leave the colony.

It was once thought that the little animals left the mountains and marched to the sea. There they were said to throw themselves into the water, where they drowned. Now scientists say that crowding and lack of food causes lemmings to leave their homes. They often die on their journey.

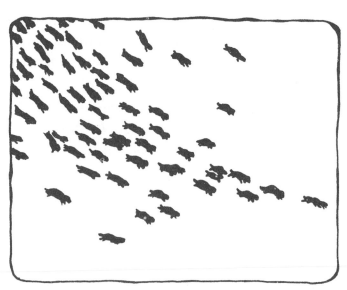

FIND THE ANSWERS

1. A colony of lemmings
   a. grows quickly.
   b. gets smaller.
   c. stays the same.
   d. grows slowly.

2. The word in the first paragraph that means *ratlike animals* is

   _____.

3. The words "They march on" in paragraph 3 tell about the

   _____.

4. The story does not say so, but it makes you think that
   a. lemmings have very few young.
   b. lemmings are hunted for their fur.
   c. lemmings could eat humans' crops.

5. Some lemmings leave the colony to find
   a. new colonies of lemmings.
   b. a place to swim.
   c. enough food to eat.

6. Lemmings live in Scandinavia.
   Yes   No   Does not say

7. On the whole, this story is about
   a. small rat colonies.
   b. why lemmings leave their homes.
   c. marching to the sea in Scandinavia.

8. Why do lemmings leave their homes?
   a. They are too crowded and lack food.
   b. It is too cold to stay in the mountains.
   c. Humans hunt them.

9. Which statement does the story lead you to believe?
   a. Lemmings stay close to their homes.
   b. There are few lemmings left.
   c. Lemmings have large families.

Favorite Foods from Far Away

Many kinds of soil and weather are found in the United States. Many different crops can be grown in our country. Oranges and grapefruit grow in southern Florida and California. The cool, damp ground of New England is right for cranberries. The plains of the Middle West are good for growing corn. The hot, sandy soil of the Southwest is right for dates.

The United States can grow almost any food that people want to buy. But there are two foods that Americans eat which will not grow here. They must be imported. Bananas and chocolate are favorite foods from far away.

Bananas grow on tree-sized plants that need heavy rain, warm weather, and rich soil. Some people who live near the southern tip of Florida raise a few bananas for their own use. But all the bananas sold in grocery stores are imported from Central America.

Chocolate and cocoa (kō′kō) are made from the seeds of the cacao (kə kā′ō) tree. This tree grows only in the warmest parts of the world. Most of our chocolate comes from South America and Africa.

Shipping costs add to the price Americans pay when they buy imported foods. Bananas and chocolate bars would cost less if banana plants and cacao trees grew in the United States.

1. In the United States, cranberries are grown in
   a. southern Florida.   c. the Middle West.
   b. California.   d. New England.

2. The word in paragraph 2 that means *shipped in from another country*

   is _____.

3. The words "favorite foods" in paragraph 2 refer to _____

   and _____.

4. The story does not say so, but it makes you think that
   a. many bananas are grown in the United States.
   b. different plants grow in different places.
   c. the United States does not import food.

5. The United States imports
   a. corn and cranberries.
   b. oranges and grapefruit.
   c. bananas and cacao seeds.

6. Cacao trees grow in the cool, damp soil of New England.
   Yes   No   Does not say

7. On the whole, this story is about
   a. foods that do not come from America.
   b. the grocery stores of South America.
   c. the shipping costs of imported foods.

8. Why do we pay high prices for bananas and chocolate?
   a. Americans do not care about the price.
   b. Not many people buy these foods.
   c. They must be shipped a long way.

9. Which statement does the story lead you to believe?
   a. The United States imports most of its food.
   b. Bananas may cost less in countries where they are grown.
   c. People in the United States could grow cacao trees if they wanted.

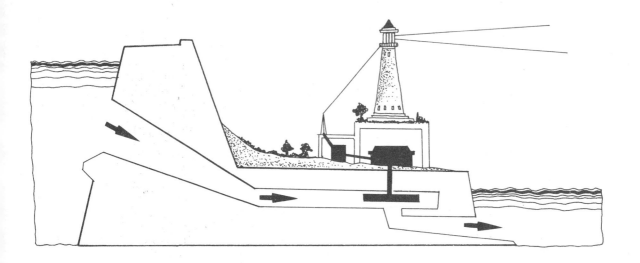

What Makes the Wheels Turn?

Every factory must have power to run its machines. How does a factory get the power it needs?

Before 1800, factories depended on water power. They were built beside waterfalls. The rushing water turned a large wooden waterwheel inside the factory. As the waterwheel turned, the wheels of the machinery also turned.

This kind of power cost little, but it could not be depended upon. If a river dried up, the waterwheel stopped turning. Often waterfalls were found in steep mountains where it was hard to build roads.

In the late 1700s, James Watt in-vented the steam engine. The steam engine used coal to make power. Then factories could be built near coal mines or wherever coal could be shipped in.

Today, most factories depend on coal, oil, or electricity for power. They must be built near coal and oil deposits or where there are dams to make electricity.

Someday, atomic plants may be built anywhere they are needed. An atomic plant uses only a small amount of fuel to make a large amount of power. But now, factories still must be near a means of power.

1. The steam engine was invented by
    a. James Watt.
    c. an atomic scientist.
    b. George Washington.
    d. a factory worker.

2. The word in paragraph 3 that means *having sharp slopes* or *tall* is

    _____.

3. The words "uses only a small amount of fuel" in the last paragraph

    describe an _____ _____.

4. The story does not say so, but it makes you think that
    a. atomic plants are built near waterfalls.
    b. new kinds of power plants are being planned.
    c. electricity will run all power plants someday.

5. Most factories today use power from
    a. coal, oil, or electricity.
    b. atomic power plants.
    c. large wooden waterwheels.

6. All factories were once built near waterfalls.
    Yes   No   Does not say

7. On the whole, this story is about
    a. machinery that is used in factories.
    b. factories in England.
    c. different kinds of power.

8. Why do factories need power?
    a. Most factories make coal, oil, or electricity.
    b. Power runs their machines.
    c. They need power to turn the waterwheels.

9. Which statement does the story lead you to believe?
    a. Water power is still used in most American factories.
    b. The steam engine used electricity to make power.
    c. Today, different factories use different kinds of power.

They Were Not Allowed To Fight

Bali (bä′lē) is a tiny island that today is part of Indonesia. It is a pretty island that has many mountains and a pleasant climate. For a long time, Bali was cut off from much of the world.

The people of Bali were happy and gay and had a peaceful way of life. They were not allowed to fight. At one time there had been terrible wars on Bali. Then the people decided it was wrong to fight and have wars. They made rules to keep apart those people who wanted to fight.

Bali was divided into seven small kingdoms. The land around each kingdom was kept empty, and no one lived there. Since the kingdoms did not share the same borders, the people could not fight about them.

On Bali, even the young were not allowed to fight. If two children started a fight over a toy, someone separated them. When two children argued, they would agree not to speak to each other. Sometimes they did not talk together for months. This gave the children a chance to forget their anger.

Families who were angry with each other also promised not to speak. Their promise was written down, and the whole village knew about it. If they broke their promise, they had to offer gifts to their gods.

FIND THE ANSWERS

1. Bali is
   a. a mountain. c. a city.
   b. a king. d. an island.

2. The word in the first paragraph that means *weather conditions* is

   _____.

3. The words "seven small kingdoms" in paragraph 3 describe

   _____.

4. The story does not say so, but it makes you think that
   a. the people of Bali worked together to keep the peace.
   b. the children on Bali could fight if they wanted.
   c. the jails in Bali are always filled with people.

5. On Bali, children were not allowed to
   a. go to school.
   b. fight with one another.
   c. live with their families.

6. Families who were angry with each other made a secret promise not to speak.
   Yes   No   Does not say

7. On the whole, this story is about
   a. a people who decided not to fight.
   b. the many wars that Bali has.
   c. the kind of toys that children have on Bali.

8. Why was the land around each kingdom kept empty?
   a. It was a good, safe place in which children could play.
   b. It was empty so that people could not fight over borders.
   c. The empty land was needed as farmland.

9. Which statement does the story lead you to believe?
   a. Bali has so few people that it is easy for them to be peaceful.
   b. The peaceful people of Bali have never had a war.
   c. People can live together in peace if they all want to.

A Dangerous Land

The cold and icy land that is the Eskimo's home is a dangerous one. The Eskimos once believed that to be safe from danger they had to obey taboos. Taboos were rules that told them what they must and must not do.

The Eskimos had taboos connected with almost everything they did. They had to keep the taboos in mind at all times. They believed that to break one would bring disaster.

For the Eskimos, it was taboo to store reindeer and seal meat together. They could not even eat the two meats on the same day. They believed the Goddess Sedna (sed′nə) had separated the land animals from the sea animals. They thought bringing these animals together would cause the hunting to be bad.

There were other taboos concerning animals. When a dead seal was brought into the house, everyone had to stop working. The spirit of the dead seal had to be given a drink of water. If it got no water, the spirit would be angered. It would keep other animals from being caught.

When the Eskimos broke a taboo, they believed a black cloud formed around their heads. They had to tell the others in the village what they had done. They did this to warn the others and to keep the black cloud from spreading bad luck through the village.

1. Eskimos live in
   a. large cities.
   b. villages.
   c. hot countries.
   d. apartments.

2. The word in paragraph 4 that means *about* or *referring to* is

   _____.

3. The words "rules that told them what they must and must not do" in the

   first paragraph describe _____.

4. The story does not say so, but it makes you think that
   a. Eskimos spent all their time eating.
   b. Eskimos believed animals had spirits.
   c. Eskimo families did not have neighbors.

5. Many Eskimo taboos concerned
   a. hunting animals.
   b. rules.
   c. the Eskimo's house.

6. Eskimos knew how to sew.
   Yes   No   Does not say

7. On the whole, this story is about
   a. the way Eskimos treated their neighbors.
   b. how the Eskimos stored their reindeer and seal meat.
   c. the things that Eskimos could and could not do.

8. Why did the Eskimos separate reindeer and seal meat?
   a. They did not have room to store both kinds of meat.
   b. They thought keeping them together caused bad hunting.
   c. The Eskimos did not eat either reindeer or seal meat.

9. Which statement does the story lead you to believe?
   a. Taboos are important to some peoples.
   b. There are many black clouds where the Eskimos live.
   c. Eskimos like land animals better than sea animals.

"Warm-Water Rivers"

In our country, power plants that make electricity are often built on rivers. Cool water that is used in making electricity becomes warm as it runs through the plant. Then the heated water is returned to the river.

When large amounts of warm water are dumped into a river, the river itself is heated. The temperature of the water may be raised only a few degrees. Yet these few degrees can change the animal and plant life in the river. Heat causes a loss of oxygen in the water. Fish no longer do well, and some kinds die. Without enough oxygen, bacteria in the river cannot break down waste matter. The river is no longer clean.

In the coming years, new power plants will be built. Many will be run by nuclear energy. A nuclear power plant heats a river even more than a power plant run by gas, oil, or coal.

In some states, laws are being passed to protect the rivers. Certain rivers will be called "cold-water rivers." Power plants will not be allowed to raise their temperature above 68° F. The temperature of "warm-water rivers" will not be raised above 83° F. Power plants will have to cool the water they pour into rivers.

FIND THE ANSWERS

1. Water that is used in making electricity
   a. flows faster.
   b. is used up.
   c. becomes warm.
   d. turns to ice.

2. The word in paragraph 2 that means *tiny plants that can only be seen through a microscope* is _____.

3. The words "warm-water" in the last paragraph describe

   _____.

4. The story does not say so, but it makes you think that
   a. fish must have oxygen.
   b. bacteria must be removed from rivers.
   c. plants need warm water.

5. Many new power plants will be run by
   a. cold-water rivers.
   b. nuclear energy.
   c. gas, coal, or oil.

6. Heat causes a loss of oxygen in rivers.
   Yes   No   Does not say

7. On the whole, this story is about
   a. the changes caused by heating rivers.
   b. how nuclear power plants use electricity.
   c. why we must build new power plants.

8. Why are laws being passed to protect our rivers?
   a. We must save all the water we can to make electricity.
   b. People are catching too many fish in our streams and rivers.
   c. Without laws, warm water dumped into rivers could kill the fish.

9. Which statement does the story lead you to believe?
   a. We will have to stop building new power plants.
   b. The animal and plant life in our rivers may change.
   c. Nobody cares about the temperatures of our rivers.

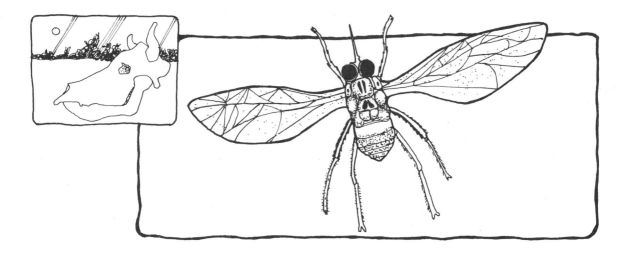

Land of the Tsetse Fly

Africa is the second largest continent in the world. Yet much of Africa has not been developed by humans into farms and cities. One of the reasons is that a dangerous and unpleasant insect called the tsetse (tset'sē) fly is found there. This fly makes its home in the heart of Africa.

The tsetse fly is a little larger than the housefly. Its name means "fly that destroys cattle." It lives by sucking blood from animals. It attacks people as well as their herds of cattle.

The tsetse fly carries sleeping sickness to those people it bites. Sleeping sickness causes illness, and some forms of it cause death. The tsetse fly also causes disease in animals. In some places in Africa, it has destroyed whole cattle herds.

It is hard for humans and their cattle to live with the tsetse fly. Some experts think that it has kept some 400,000 square miles of Africa a wilderness. This wilderness is a place as large as the whole United States.

Without the tsetse fly, more land could be used by humans. Without it, many more cattle could be raised. People are working to get rid of the fly. However, it is a hard job that will take a long time.

1. The tsetse fly lives in
   a. the United States.
   b. Africa.
   c. Asia.
   d. Europe.

2. The word in the first paragraph that means *made useful* or *made usable* is _____.

3. The words "it has destroyed whole cattle herds" in paragraph 3 refer to _____ _____.

4. The story does not say so, but it makes you think that
   a. tsetse flies would also attack horses.
   b. the tsetse fly is known as a human's friend.
   c. Africa is a well-developed land.

5. Sleeping sickness is
   a. a kind of cattle.
   b. the name of a wilderness.
   c. a disease.

6. The tsetse fly sucks blood from animals.
   Yes   No   Does not say

7. On the whole, this story is about
   a. the second largest continent in the world.
   b. a dangerous and unpleasant insect.
   c. farmland in the heart of Africa.

8. Why is the tsetse fly a problem in Africa?
   a. People do not like the buzzing sound it makes.
   b. It eats food that humans need.
   c. It has killed many cattle herds.

9. Which statement does the story lead you to believe?
   a. It will be easy to get rid of the tsetse flies in Africa.
   b. Africa is at least as large as the United States.
   c. Sleeping sickness is unknown in Africa.

Diving into Danger

The sea has always interested people. From it they can get food, minerals, and treasures. For thousands of years, they sailed on the sea. But they could not go far beneath its surface.

People want to explore deep into the sea. However, they are not fishes. Because people must breathe air, they cannot stay under the water's surface for any length of time. To explore deep water, men and women face even more dangers and problems.

A diver who wants to stay under water for more than a few minutes must breathe air or a special mixture of gases. Divers can wear diving suits and have air pumped to them from above. They can carry tanks of air on their back and breathe through a hose and a mouthpiece.

Water weighs 800 times as much as air. Tons of water push against a diver deep in the sea. The diver's body is under great pressure.

When divers are under great pressure, their blood takes in some of the gases they breathe. As they rise to the surface, the water pressure becomes less. If the divers rise too quickly, the gases in their blood form bubbles. Divers then suffer from the bends. The bends can cause divers to double up in pain. Bends can even kill divers.

1. A diver's body in deep water
    a. is under great pressure.
    b. is just like a fish's body.
    c. suffers from the bends.
    d. weighs very little.

2. The word in paragraph 3 that means *a blend* is _____.

3. The words "under great pressure" in paragraph 4 describe a diver's

    _____.

4. The story does not say so, but it makes you think that
    a. deep-sea divers should be in good health.
    b. divers explore the deep seas only for treasure.
    c. diving under the water too quickly causes the bends.

5. The gases in a diver's blood can form
    a. great pressure.
    b. air.
    c. bubbles.

6. Water weighs twice as much as air.
    Yes   No   Does not say

7. On the whole, this story is about
    a. special mixtures of gases.
    b. the problems of deep-sea diving.
    c. air pressure.

8. Why do divers get the bends?
    a. They try to do exercises under the water.
    b. Their diving suits weigh too much.
    c. They come to the surface too quickly.

9. Which statement does the story lead you to believe?
    a. The sea began to interest humans in the last few years.
    b. Humans are not at home deep in the sea.
    c. All divers get the bends sooner or later.

Evil Spirits Lived There

Today, humans have reached the top of the world's highest mountains. But for many years, even people who lived in the mountains did not climb them. Indeed, people believed that they could not climb mountains.

For a long time, mountains were thought to be the home of evil spirits. People believed dragons lived on the mountainside. They thought these dragons would gobble up anyone coming near.

When humans began to climb mountains, they faced many dangers. The air high on a mountain was freezing cold. There were deep cracks into which a climber could fall. Roaring winds and terrible storms could sweep people off the mountainside.

At first, humans did not have the proper equipment to climb high mountains. They did not have ice axes, ropes, or the right kind of clothing.

Later, mountain climbers could not reach the top of the highest peaks for another reason. As they climbed higher, the air became thinner. There was less oxygen to breathe. Above 18,000 feet, climbers had to stop every few steps to catch their breath. Their hearts beat faster, and their blood became thick. Above 25,000 feet, a climber would begin to see things that were not there. It became hard to think clearly about what must be done.

1. Mountains were once thought to be the home of
   a. roaring winds.   c. terrible storms.
   b. many insects.   d. evil spirits.

2. The word in paragraph 2 that means *to eat fast* is _____.

3. The words "who lived in the mountains" in the first paragraph refer

   to _____.

4. The story does not say so, but it makes you think that
   a. people who lived in the mountains always climbed them.
   b. some people still would not want to climb a mountain.
   c. humans no longer face dangers when they climb mountains.

5. In high mountains, there is less
   a. snow and ice.
   b. oxygen to breathe.
   c. wind.

6. Humans cannot climb mountains above 50,000 feet.
   Yes   No   Does not say

7. On the whole, this story is about
   a. the dangers of climbing high mountains.
   b. the evil spirits and dragons that live on mountains.
   c. the proper equipment needed to climb mountains.

8. Why didn't people climb mountains long ago?
   a. It was too cold on the mountains.
   b. It was hard to breathe in the mountains.
   c. They were afraid of spirits and dragons.

9. Which statement does the story lead you to believe?
   a. Mountain climbing can be a dangerous sport.
   b. The air in the high mountains is very thick.
   c. Dragons once ate people who tried to climb mountains.

A Passport to Travel

All governments have laws, or rules, that must be followed by their citizens. Many laws are made to protect people. Some of the rules that our government has made are about travel.

Americans can travel almost anywhere they choose. But to protect its citizens, our government lists a few places where Americans cannot go. These places are unfriendly countries and countries at war. There, the traveler might not be safe. These countries are listed in a small book called a passport.

This passport is a government's request for the safety of its traveling citizen. It is also a government's pledge that the citizen will respect the rules of the host country.

To receive passports from the government, travelers must prove they are United States citizens. An American cannot go overseas without a passport. Only certain nearby countries such as Canada and Mexico do not ask for passports.

Pasted inside the passport is the traveler's picture. Children traveling with their parents are included in one parent's book.

Thousands of people from the United States visit other countries every year. An American traveler might carry plane tickets, money, clothing, and many other things. But the most important thing a traveler carries in another country is a passport.

1. Americans can travel
   a. to unfriendly countries.
   b. almost anywhere.
   c. only to Canada and Mexico.
   d. only to close countries.

2. The word in paragraph 3 that means *obey* or *follow* is

   _____.

3. The words "a small book" in paragraph 2 describe a _____.

4. The story does not say so, but it makes you think that
   a. children cannot travel overseas.
   b. a traveler is not safe in most countries.
   c. Americans like to travel.

5. A passport is not needed when an American goes to
   a. dangerous places.
   b. Canada or Mexico.
   c. countries overseas.

6. American citizens must respect the rules of the host country.
   Yes   No   Does not say

7. On the whole, this story is about
   a. the rules one must follow when going overseas.
   b. traveling in nearby countries such as Canada and Mexico.
   c. the governments of countries overseas.

8. Why do travelers need passports?
   a. They need something more to carry when they travel.
   b. They help our country to protect its citizens.
   c. They need to have their pictures taken more often.

9. Which statement does the story lead you to believe?
   a. People should take good care of their passports.
   b. It is not important to have a passport to travel.
   c. Children are never included on a passport.

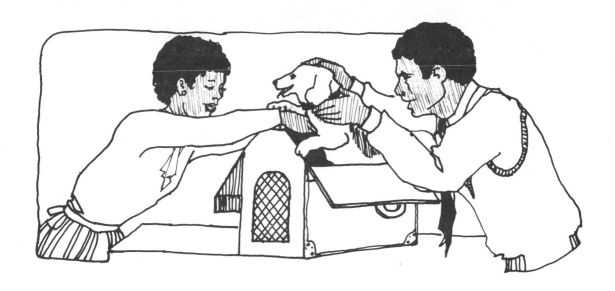

Traveling Animals

Animals traveling from one country to another have to follow laws, just as people do. They do not have to have passports, but they have to obey other rules. Most countries have laws about animals coming into their country. The laws were made to stop the spread of diseases that animals carry.

Traveling animals include cats and dogs going with their masters on trips. Others are rare animals going to zoos. Some are birds and fish on their way to pet shops.

Some animals cannot go into a country unless their owners can prove that they have been vaccinated against certain diseases. Others must be studied carefully by animal doctors.

Sometimes animals must spend a month or more in a special place before they can enter a country. The animals are fenced in. There, they are kept away from other animals until it is certain that they do not have a disease. Only the people who care for the animals can go near.

There are many different laws in each country. Anyone who wants to take a pet to another country should check with the government first. Laws are made to protect both people and animals.

1. Animals that travel have to
   a. have passports.
   b. travel with masters.
   c. follow rules and laws.
   d. see a dentist.

2. The word in paragraph 2 that means *not often found* is

   _____ .

3. The words "cats and dogs" in paragraph 2 refer to traveling

   _____ .

4. The story does not say so, but it makes you think that
   a. there are special doctors who treat only animals.
   b. animal owners cannot take their pets on trips.
   c. when an animal is ill, its owner must take it home.

5. Animals are often vaccinated against
   a. some kinds of rules.
   b. certain diseases.
   c. their masters.

6. Different countries have different laws about traveling animals.
   Yes   No   Does not say

7. On the whole, this story is about
   a. ways to stop the spread of diseases that animals carry.
   b. birds and fish on their way to pet shops in our country.
   c. cats and dogs going with their masters on overseas trips.

8. Why are some animals kept in a special place before entering a country?
   a. Their masters are trying to sell them.
   b. They must be checked for disease.
   c. They are waiting for passports.

9. Which statement does the story lead you to believe?
   a. Animals are fenced in while they travel.
   b. People who care for animals carry diseases.
   c. Many people take their pets on trips.

Walls of Concrete

Today, we are used to seeing many kinds of buildings. Some houses are only one story high, while an office building might rise twenty floors into the sky. Builders use many kinds of materials. They can select wood, stone, glass, brick, or metal for use in a building.

Centuries ago, people did not have many building materials. Their tools were also limited. Most of the buildings put up in a country looked alike.

The Romans were well known for huge buildings that had thick walls and small, narrow windows. One of these buildings was the Pantheon (pan'thē on) in Rome. Built nearly 2,000 years ago, the building was so strong that it is still used as a church. This round building can hold 3,000 people.

The Romans knew how to make concrete and used it in building arches and domes. To support their heavy arches, the Romans had to build strong walls. The walls of the Pantheon are 20 feet thick. There are few windows because openings would weaken the walls.

For over a thousand years, public buildings in Europe were built with Roman arches and domes. Until 1100, other peoples copied the Roman way of building. Concrete was the best material people knew about for making large buildings.

1. The Romans knew how to make
    a. office buildings.
    b. metal.   ,
    c. apartment houses.
    d. concrete.

2. The word in paragraph 4 that means *to hold up* is _____.

3. The words "looked alike" in paragraph 2 describe the

    _____.

4. The story does not say so, but it makes you think that
    a. Roman buildings were rather dark inside.
    b. people in Europe did not like Roman buildings.
    c. builders today must make their buildings of concrete.

5. The Pantheon has
    a. many large windows.
    b. only a few narrow windows.
    c. no windows at all.

6. Centuries ago, people used the same materials we use today.
    Yes   No   Does not say

7. On the whole, this story is about
    a. the Roman way of building.
    b. public buildings in Europe.
    c. office buildings made of glass.

8. Why did the Romans have to build thick, strong walls?
    a. They wanted other peoples to copy their buildings.
    b. They needed protection from their enemies.
    c. The arches of their buildings were very heavy.

9. Which statement does the story lead you to believe?
    a. Many years ago, buildings in a country did not look alike.
    b. Roman buildings were very well built.
    c. The Romans liked to make their buildings out of wood.

Buildings Full of Light

Roman buildings were popular only as long as builders were limited in how tall they could make a building. They had not learned how to support the walls of a tall building.

About 1140, a new kind of building

appeared in Europe. These new buildings were churches, or cathedrals, and they were seen first in France. Today, these cathedrals are called Gothic buildings. Their pointed arches rise toward the sky. They look very different from the Roman buildings that have low arches and thick walls. Unlike the dark Pantheon, these tall buildings are full of light.

Builders of the Gothic cathedrals found a new way to build strong walls and tall arches. They built supports outside the building. These supports, called "flying buttresses," helped hold up the walls. Buttresses made it possible to build higher buildings.

One end of a narrow beam, or the flying buttress, was planted away from the wall. The other end was placed high up on the wall. The flying buttress acted like a crutch.

Since these buildings had many windows, artists made pictures in them by using small pieces of colored glass held together with lead. Sunlight streamed through the glass and made soft splashes of color inside the churches. Stained glass windows and flying buttresses were part of every Gothic cathedral.

1. Gothic cathedrals were first seen
   - a. in Russia.
   - b. in China.
   - c. in France.
   - d. in the United States.

2. The word in paragraph 4 that means *prop* or *support* is

   _____.

3. The words "that have low arches and thick walls" in paragraph 2

   describe the Roman _____.

4. The story does not say so, but it makes you think that
   - a. stained glass windows supported Gothic buildings.
   - b. flying buttresses were used only for decoration.
   - c. tall buildings needed extra support for their walls.

5. The windows of Gothic cathedrals
   - a. were made of colored glass.
   - b. were very thick.
   - c. were like those in Roman buildings.

6. Gothic buildings were much taller than Roman buildings.
   Yes   No   Does not say

7. On the whole, this story is about
   - a. how to make stained glass windows.
   - b. the Pantheon.
   - c. Gothic cathedrals.

8. Why didn't the Romans build tall buildings?
   - a. They liked low, round buildings better.
   - b. They had not learned how to support the walls.
   - c. They did not want to use flying buttresses.

9. Which statement does the story lead you to believe?
   - a. Roman buildings had no outside supports.
   - b. Roman buildings had large stained glass windows.
   - c. Roman buildings looked much like Gothic buildings.

The Curious Brother
(A Norse Folktale)

Once upon a time there were three brothers. Jack, the youngest, wondered about things and asked many questions. His brothers poked fun at him and said, "Oh, Jack, you're a fool to be so curious."

One day, a stranger came to the cottage where the three brothers lived. He told them that the King who lived close by had a great oak tree growing near his palace. The oak blocked the light from the King's windows, and he wanted the tree chopped down. However, with each ax blow, the tree only grew larger.

The King also wanted someone to dig a well and fill it with water. But no one could dig through the rock on which the palace stood.

The King said he would not rest until these tasks were done. He promised half his kingdom and his daughter's hand in marriage to the man who could do them.

When Jack and his brothers heard this story, they decided to try their luck. So they set off for the King's palace.

After a time, the three brothers sat down to rest in a shady woods. In the distance, they could hear a loud noise among the trees. Jack said, "I wonder what that noise is."

His brothers said, "How silly you are! It's probably a woodcutter chopping down a tree."

But Jack was curious, and he wanted to find out for himself. Jack followed the sound until he came to an ax that was chopping away at a large pine tree. Jack was surprised to see an ax that could chop by itself.

50

He took the ax and put it in a pack he carried on his back.

When Jack returned, his brothers asked him what he had seen. "Only an ax," Jack said.

Soon the brothers came to a rocky hill. They could hear the noise of someone digging at the top.

Jack said, "I wonder what is digging at the top of that hill."

His brothers laughed. "It is just some animal digging a burrow," they said.

But Jack was not satisfied with that answer. He said, "I think I'll climb that hill and see for myself."

When Jack got to the top, he was surprised to find a shovel digging in the earth by itself. He took the shovel, removed its handle, and put the parts into his pack. Then he returned to his brothers.

Jack's brothers asked him what had been doing the digging. "Only a shovel," Jack answered.

The brothers continued walking until they saw a pretty stream rushing along. Jack said to his brothers, "Don't you wonder where all this water is coming from?"

His brothers said, "Jack, you could drive a person crazy with all your questions! The stream must come from a spring in the earth."

But Jack said, "I think I'll find out." Jack followed the stream until he saw that it trickled from a hole in a large walnut. Jack plugged up the hole with a small stone. Then he put the walnut in his pack and went back to his brothers.

Jack's brothers asked him where the water came from. "Out of a hole," said Jack.

The next day, the three brothers found themselves at the King's palace. The oldest brother was the first to try to chop down the great oak. But try as he might, the tree only grew bigger with each blow of his ax. Then the second brother took a turn, but he had no better luck.

At last Jack stepped forward. His brothers cried out, "If we couldn't chop down this great oak, how can a foolish boy like you?"

Jack took the ax from his pack. "Ax," he said, "chop down this tree." Before long, the ax had chopped down the tree.

Next Jack took out the shovel and put it back together. "Shovel," he said, "dig the King his well." Soon the shovel had dug a deep well.

Then Jack took the walnut from his pack. He pulled out the stone which held back the water, and he laid the walnut in the well. "Walnut, fill the well," he said. Soon the well was gushing with water.

The King was very pleased. His oak had been chopped down and he had a well with all the water he could wish. Jack married the King's daughter and got half the kingdom.

Jack's brothers could only shake their heads sadly and say, "Perhaps our curious brother was not such a fool after all."

748 words

II

The Use of Earth, Space, and Materials Depends On the Needs of the Users

In this section you will read about the use of earth, space, and materials dependent on the needs of the users. You will read about these things from the standpoint of space, history, biology, economics, anthropology, geography, earth science, political science, and art.

Keep these questions in mind when you are reading.

1. Are the needs of all people the same?

2. If not, what causes needs of people to differ?

3. Will all people need to use the same materials to meet their needs?

4. Do the different needs of people affect the way they live?

5. If all people do not need the same materials, what happens to the materials left over?

A Rock with Three Names

Meteroid, *meteor*, and *meteorite* are words that describe the same thing. They describe the pieces of rock or metal that come from outer space. But each word is used at a different time.

A meteoroid is a piece of matter moving in space. Meteoroids move as fast as 40 miles a second. Made up of iron or stone, they may be large or small. Most of them are smaller than grains of sand. When the spacecraft *Mariner IV* flew past Mars in 1965, it was hit 200 times by meteoroids.

As a meteoroid comes into the air near the earth, it catches fire. The flash of light from the burning meteoroid is called a meteor. Most meteoroids burn up before they hit the earth. If a piece of meteoroid falls to the ground, it is called a meteorite.

People have studied these rocks from space for many years. They now have a new interest in them. They need to find ways to keep meteoroids from making holes in spacecraft and harming the people inside.

Thick walls may help. Perhaps the spacecraft can be covered with metal skin that will seal itself. Some automobile tires in use today are self-sealing. In the same way, a self-sealing skin might keep a spacecraft safe.

1. Someday, spacecraft may be covered with
   a. automobile tires.   c. meteorites.
   b. self-sealing metal skins. d. flashes of light.

2. The word in the first paragraph that means *far away* is

   _____.

3. The words "a piece of matter moving in space" in paragraph 2 describe

   a _____.

4. The story does not say so, but it makes you think that
   a. many people in spacecraft have been harmed by meteoroids.
   b. meteoroids will have to be removed from the sky.
   c. spacecraft cannot steer clear of all meteoroids.

5. Meteoroids are made up of
   a. air and gases.
   b. grains of sand.
   c. iron or stone.

6. *Mariner IV* was hit by meteoroids thousands of times.
   Yes   No   Does not say

7. On the whole, this story is about
   a. meteoroids and spacecraft in outer space.
   b. some uses for self-sealing automobile tires.
   c. the speed with which meteoroids travel.

8. Why are people so interested in meteoroids now?
   a. They want to find ways to stop meteoroids from harming space-craft.
   b. They want to know more about light flashes in outer space.
   c. They want to describe the rocks from outer space.

9. Which statement does the story lead you to believe?
   a. A meteor can be described as a piece of rock.
   b. Some meteorites have been found on the earth.
   c. All meteoroids burn up before they hit the ground.

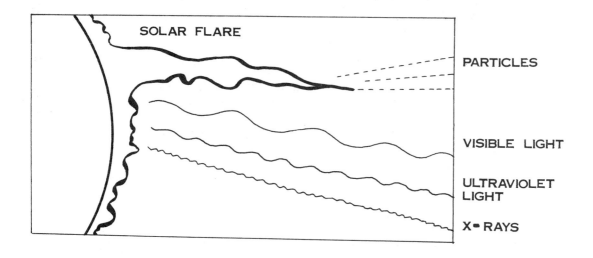

SOLAR FLARE

PARTICLES

VISIBLE LIGHT

ULTRAVIOLET LIGHT

X-RAYS

Danger in the Sky

The sun is our most important star. It can be dangerous to humans both here on earth and in outer space. We need to find out all we can about its dangers.

Many stars are larger than our sun. However, the sun is about 250,000 times closer to the earth than any other star. Most of our energy comes from the sun's rays. We can trace electricity, wind, water power, and even the energy in our bodies back to the sun.

Not all kinds of solar rays reach the earth. The earth is wrapped in a blanket of air that keeps out rays that might harm us. Now people are exploring space. They are going out-side their blanket of air. They have become interested in the dangerous solar rays.

Sometimes there are storms in the sun's hot gases. These storms are called solar flares. During solar flares, the sun puts out heavy rays that move at faster speeds than usual. The rays can make spacecraft engines break down. They might cause people in space to become ill or die.

There is no way to tell when a solar flare will take place. Before it is safe for humans to go on long trips through space, we need to know more about solar flares. We must find better ways to protect people from the sun's dangerous rays.

1. The storms caused by the sun's hot gases are called
   a. heavy rays.
   b. blankets of air.
   c. solar flares.
   d. dust storms.

2. The word in paragraph 4 that means *flames* or *blazes* is

   _____ .

3. The words "their blanket of air" in paragraph 3 refer to

   _____ .

4. The story does not say so, but it makes you think that
   a. the sun's rays are not important to us.
   b. dangerous solar rays do not reach the earth.
   c. solar flares are caused by electricity.

5. The earth is wrapped in
   a. a blanket of air.
   b. solar rays.
   c. dangerous solar flares.

6. The sun is our largest star.
   Yes   No   Does not say

7. On the whole, this story is about
   a. spacecraft going to the sun.
   b. the sun's dangerous rays.
   c. electricity, wind, and water power.

8. Why are people going outside their blanket of air?
   a. They are tired of the earth.
   b. They want to each the sun.
   c. They want to explore outer space.

9. Which statement does the story lead you to believe?
   a. Humans could not live on earth without the sun's help.
   b. Storms on the sun are like storms on earth.
   c. Solar rays help spacecraft engines move faster.

Listening to the Stars

Karl Jansky was a young engineer who worked for a telephone company. In 1931, he was given a hard task. His company told him that it needed to know why so much noise, or static, came over its telephone lines. People could not hear over the roar.

To find the answer, Jansky built a funny-looking antenna. He hoped the antenna would find the cause of the static. Up to that time, everyone believed that static came from thunderstorms. Jansky discovered that some of the static did, indeed, come from storms, both near and far. But one kind of static was always there and was not caused by thunderstorms. This static came from stars far out in space. Radio waves given off by the stars caused the static.

Other people wanted to study these waves, too. They built other large antennas. The new antennas were the first radio telescopes.

Today, radio telescopes are used to make new maps of the sky. Using them, scientists have found groups of stars that were too far away to be seen with other telescopes. Radio telescopes can be used night and day and in all kinds of weather.

Radio telescopes have another important use. They can be used to track rockets and spacecraft as they circle the earth or climb out into space.

1. Long ago, people believed that all static came from
   - a. outer space.
   - b. thunderstorms.
   - c. large antennas.
   - d. stars in space.

2. The word in the first paragraph that means *electric noises* is

   _____ .

3. The words "the first radio telescopes" in paragraph 3 describe the new

   _____ .

4. The story does not say so, but it makes you think that
   - a. Karl Jansky was given an easy task.
   - b. all static comes from stars far out in space.
   - c. telephone lines carry less static now than in the past.

5. Today, radio telescopes are used to
   - a. find the cause of static.
   - b. stop static.
   - c. make maps of the sky.

6. Some static does come from thunderstorms.
   Yes   No   Does not say

7. On the whole, this story is about
   - a. radio waves and radio telescopes.
   - b. static that comes over TV sets.
   - c. rockets and spacecraft.

8. Why are today's radio telescopes better than the first telescopes?
   - a. They stop bad thunderstorms.
   - b. They can be used anytime.
   - c. They can be used in any radio.

9. Which statement does the story lead you to believe?
   - a. People in rockets and spacecraft make new maps of the sky.
   - b. Many new stars have been discovered since 1931.
   - c. Karl Jansky was the only one interested in radio waves.

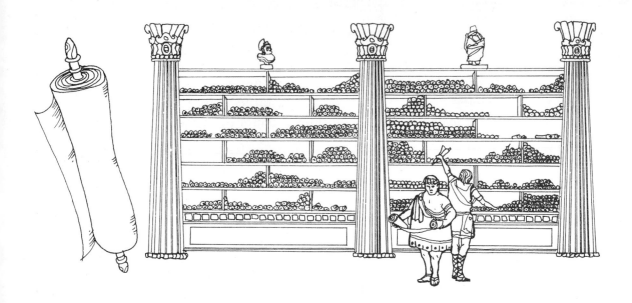

The Library at Alexandria

Long ago, in 331 B.C., Greece conquered Egypt and built Alexandria. This city was named after Alexander the Great, King of Greece. After Alexander's death, a Greek general named Ptolemy (tol'ə mē) became ruler of Egypt.

The Greeks loved learning. Ptolemy believed that people needed to have written records of their thoughts and ideas. They needed to have a place to collect their books. For the first time in history, Ptolemy tried to collect together all the Greek books that had been written. To do this, he built the largest and best library in the ancient world.

Before this time, great writings were often hard to find, and many had been lost. Books then were written by hand on a kind of paper called papyrus. Sheets of papyrus were rolled around wooden sticks. The papyrus rolls were stored in deep shelves on the library walls.

All books brought into Egypt were taken to the library. There, scholars studied them and corrected any mistakes. The books were copied over so they would be easier to read and store. They were listed in a catalog.

The library at Alexandria grew to have over half a million books. It was a center of learning for over 700 years before it was destroyed by fire in A.D. 391.

1. Ptolemy was a
   - a. writer.
   - b. King of Greece.
   - c. Greek general.
   - d. doctor.

2. The word in paragraph 4 that means *people with much learning* is

   _____ .

3. The words "written by hand" in paragraph 3 refer to _____ .

4. The story does not say so, but it makes you think that
   - a. copying books by hand took a long time.
   - b. it was hard to make papyrus.
   - c. no one ever read the books at Alexandria.

5. Books brought into Ptolemy's library were
   - a. written in French.
   - b. listed in a catalog.
   - c. owned by the King of Greece.

6. In 331 B.C., most Egyptians knew how to read.

   Yes   No   Does not say

7. On the whole, this story is about
   - a. an early library built by Ptolemy.
   - b. storing rolls of papyrus.
   - c. correcting the mistakes in early books.

8. Why did Ptolemy build a large library at Alexandria?
   - a. He thought it would make him as famous as Alexander the Great.
   - b. He wanted a safe place to collect all Greek books.
   - c. He wanted to find a new way to print books.

9. Which statement does the story lead you to believe?
   - a. The library at Alexandria only had a few hundred books.
   - b. There were many libraries all over Egypt.
   - c. The great library helped make Alexandria famous.

A Bathtub Made of Clay

People have always needed ways to get fresh water for drinking and washing. They have also needed ways to get rid of waste water. That is why the first plumbing systems were built thousands of years ago.

Crete is an island in the Mediterranean Sea. In 1600 B.C., a great palace stood on Crete. The palace had fresh water, toilets, baths, drains, and sewers. It may also have had a hot-water system.

The Cretans used well-fitted clay pipes to bring fresh water to the palace rooms from faraway springs. Stone drains carried away rainwater from the roof and open courts into deep sewers. These sewers were so large that a person could walk inside them.

The palace even had stone toilets. They were flushed by rainwater that flowed through the pipes or by water poured in.

The Queen of Crete had her own apartment in the palace with her own bathroom. Her clay bathtub looked much like bathtubs do today. It was painted inside with pictures of tall water grasses. Servants filled the tub with water brought from a nearby room. They emptied the bath water into a drain in the floor near the tub.

The ruins of the palace still stand. Visitors can see yet the ancient plumbing system that was not equaled until modern times.

1. Water was brought to the palace by
   a. many servants.
   c. natural streams.
   b. clay pipes.
   d. stone tubes.

2. The word in the first paragraph that means *a system of pipes* is

   _____.

3. The words "a person could walk inside them" in paragraph 3 refer to

   the _____.

4. The story does not say so, but it makes you think that
   a. the Cretans did not have very good plumbing.
   b. everyone in the palace used the same bathtub.
   c. plumbing is not a modern idea.

5. The Queen's bathtub
   a. had a drain in the center.
   b. was large and square.
   c. had pictures painted inside.

6. Even the ruins of the palace at Crete have disappeared now.
   Yes   No   Does not say

7. On the whole, this story is about
   a. plumbing in ancient Crete.
   b. painting pictures in bathtubs.
   c. the Mediterranean Sea.

8. Why did the Cretans build drains?
   a. The drains brought in fresh water.
   b. The drains carried away rain and waste water.
   c. They needed some work to do.

9. Which statement does the story lead you to believe?
   a. Crete's plumbing system was the best in the ancient world.
   b. In 1600 B.C., it was impossible to have a hot-water system.
   c. The people of Crete brought drinking water from the Mediterranean.

All Roads Lead to Rome

Over 2,000 years ago, Rome was the center of a large empire. The Romans needed a way to move their large armies quickly so they could protect their huge country. They needed land trade routes. So they joined all the parts of their empire by a network of roads.

Beginning in 300 B.C., the Romans built roads in Europe, Asia, and North Africa. By A.D. 200, they had built 50,000 miles of almost straight highways.

To build their fine highways, the Romans began by removing all soft soil. They dug until they reached hard ground. Then they added layers of stone and cement. The most important roads were paved with large, flat stones. Main Roman roads were sometimes as wide as our three-lane highways.

To build their roads, the Romans sometimes had to dig tunnels through mountains. They did not have explosives to cut through rock. They heated the rock with fire and then threw cold water over it. When the rock cracked, they dug it out with hand tools.

Roman soldiers and slaves built the roads without powerful machinery. They had only simple tools, such as shovels and picks. Yet the roads were so well built that they were used for hundreds of years.

FIND THE ANSWERS

1. Romans paved their most important roads with
   a. sand.   c. gravel.
   b. hard soil.   d. flat stones.

2. The word in the first paragraph that means *several countries that have one ruler* is _____.

3. The words "wide as our three-lane highways" in paragraph 3 describe the main Roman _____.

4. The story does not say so, but it makes you think that
   a. building roads without machinery was an easy job.
   b. it took a long time for the Romans to build roads by hand.
   c. the United States still uses the old Roman way of building roads.

5. To build tunnels for mountain roads, the Romans
   a. used explosives to break through the rock.
   b. cracked the rock with fire and cold water.
   c. dug through the rock with machinery.

6. The Romans had to rebuild their roads every few years.
   Yes   No   Does not say

7. On the whole, this story is about
   a. our modern road-building methods.
   b. Roman tools and machinery.
   c. how the Romans built highways.

8. Why did the Romans build so many roads?
   a. Their soldiers needed something to do.
   b. They did not know how to sail boats.
   c. They needed land trade routes.

9. Which statement does the story lead you to believe?
   a. Soft soil does not make a solid base for a road.
   b. The Romans built roads only on flat land.
   c. Flat stones were used only in roads in Asia.

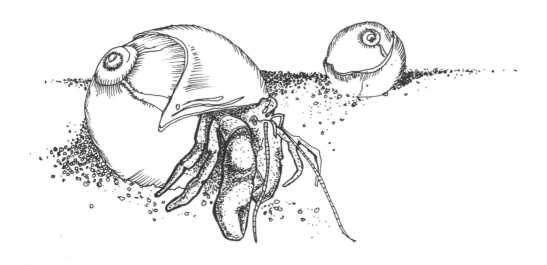

A Seashell Is Its House

A hermit crab does not have a hard shell as most crabs do. Its long, soft body makes a nice meal for a hungry fish. It needs a way to protect itself. So it moves into the empty shell of a snail or other sea animal.

The hermit crab lives safely inside its borrowed house. Only its legs and eyes stick out from the shell opening. It can move around with its house on its back and still see where it is going.

The hermit crab has only one problem. The shell cannot grow in size as the crab grows larger. There comes a time when its house is too small.

The hermit crab must keep its old home until it finds another. But finding the right home is not always easy. The crab is like a person shopping for a new coat. It must make sure it gets one that fits properly.

When the hermit crab sees a shell that looks right, it leaves its old one. It backs into the new seashell and tries it on for size. If it is too large, a fish might pull the crab out. If it picks a house that is too snug, it will not be comfortable. The hermit crab searches until it finds a house that is just right.

1. Most crabs are protected by
   a. small fish.   c. hard shells.
   b. fishers.   d. snails.

2. The word in the last paragraph that means *at ease* is

   _____ .

3. The words "It needs a way to protect itself" in paragraph 1 describe the

   _____ _____ .

4. The story does not say so, but it makes you think that
   a. the hermit crab does not live in a shell.
   b. most crabs grow new shells when their body grows.
   c. strong fish can pull hermit crabs out of tight shells.

5. The hermit crab's shell
   a. keeps it from moving.
   b. must fit properly.
   c. grows as the crab grows.

6. It is always easy for the hermit crab to find a new home.
   Yes   No   Does not say

7. On the whole, this story is about
   a. the hermit crab's borrowed shells.
   b. how hungry fish find food.
   c. how to shop for a new coat.

8. Why does the hermit crab have to look for a new home?
   a. Its body gets too large for its shell.
   b. It gets tired of its old shell.
   c. The old shell begins to crack and fall apart.

9. Which statement does the story lead you to believe?
   a. Hermit crabs pick large shells for new homes.
   b. The hermit crab's borrowed shell is never comfortable.
   c. A shell protects the hermit crab from its enemies.

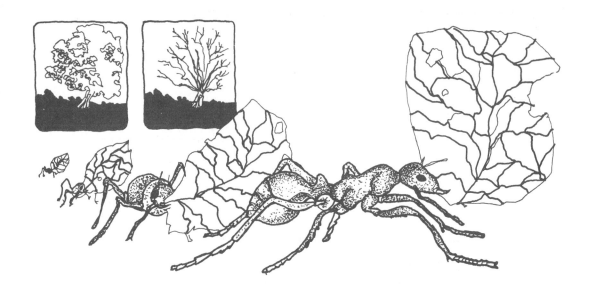

Farmers of the Ant World

Many leaf-cutter ants live in the jungles of Central and South America. Their favorite food is a kind of fungus that does not grow wild. The ants need to raise it in gardens deep in their underground nests.

Like human farmers, the leaf-cutters work hard. First they clear roads leading from the nest entrance to nearby trees. Then they pull leaves from trees and drop or carry them to the ground.

They cut the leaves into large pieces. Each ant carries a piece of leaf larger than itself back to the nest. With leaves rising from their jaws, the ants are hidden. Marching in single file, they look like a parade of walking leaves.

The leaves are brought into the nest. There, ants chew them up and spit them out. The chewed leaves become the soil on which the ants plant their gardens.

It takes much care to grow the fungus. Worker ants keep the gardens weeded. To keep the climate in the nest just right, they close or open tunnels that let in air from outside.

When a queen starts a new nest, she takes a bit of fungus with her. In this way, every nest has its own garden.

1. The leaf-cutter ant's favorite food is
      a. tree leaves.   c. wild flowers.
      b. a kind of fungus.   d. a kind of berry.

2. The word in paragraph 2 that means *a way to go in* is _____.

3. The words "they look like a parade of walking leaves" in paragraph 3

   describe the _____.

4. The story does not say so, but it makes you think that
      a. not all leaf-cutter ants have the same job.
      b. leaf-cutter ants build their nests in trees.
      c. growing fungus is very easy work.

5. Leaf-cutter ants carry pieces of leaves
      a. by dragging them along the ground.
      b. between their front legs.
      c. in their jaws.

6. Leaf-cutter ants raise fungus on old rotten logs.
      Yes   No   Does not say

7. On the whole, this story is about
      a. South American jungles.
      b. how leaf-cutter ants grow fungus.
      c. marching in single file.

8. Why does the queen take fungus to a new nest?
      a. She is hungry and will need something to eat.
      b. The new nest will need a fungus garden.
      c. The fungus helps the other ants to follow her.

9. Which statement does the story lead you to believe?
      a. Leaf-cutter ants work together to grow their food.
      b. Leaf-cutter ants hide under piles of dead leaves.
      c. Leaf-cutter ants eat different kinds of leaves.

Artists of the Bird World

Among some kinds of birds, the males are brightly decorated with head crests or fancy tail feathers. Their beautiful colors help them attract mates.

But the coloring of the male bowerbirds is dull and plain. They do not have crests or fancy feathers. They need some way to attract mates. So they build and show off small houses called bowers.

The satin bowerbird of Australia builds his bower of twigs and leaves. Shaped like a tunnel, it is large enough for the male to dance and play inside. He can enter or leave through openings at both ends.

A male decorates his bower with bright and interesting treasures. He uses flowers, toadstools, shells, stones, feathers, and fruits. If he finds a bottle cap or silver coin, he uses that, too. He may lay bright objects in heaps around the bower. He may hang some on the walls, just as people hang pictures in their houses. If some object does not match the others, he removes and hides it.

Sometimes a bowerbird paints the inside walls with colored berry juice. For a brush, he uses a piece of bark or a leaf.

There are about twenty kinds of bowerbirds. Because of their remarkable bowers, they are called the artists and engineers of the bird world.

1. A bowerbird attracts a mate with
   a. a head crest.
   b. a long tail.
   c. a fancy bower.
   d. beautiful songs.

2. The word in the last paragraph that means *outstanding* or *unusual* is

   _____.

3. The words "the coloring . . . is dull and plain" in paragraph 2

   describe the male _____.

4. The story does not say so, but it makes you think that
   a. male bowerbirds have beautiful feathers.
   b. not all bowerbirds build the same kind of bower.
   c. female bowerbirds build their own nests.

5. A bower built by a satin bowerbird
   a. is made of twigs and leaves.
   b. is made of feathers.
   c. is painted bright blue.

6. The female bowerbird lays eggs in the bower.
   Yes   No   Does not say

7. On the whole, this story is about
   a. how bowerbirds build their bowers.
   b. artists and engineers.
   c. treasures found in tunnels.

8. Why are bowerbirds called the artists and engineers of the bird world?
   a. They paint pictures of shells and stones.
   b. They build such beautiful bowers.
   c. They like to build long tunnels.

9. Which statement does the story lead you to believe?
   a. Bowerbirds spend all their time dancing.
   b. Bowerbirds paint with the tips of their wings.
   c. Female bowerbirds are attracted by pretty bowers.

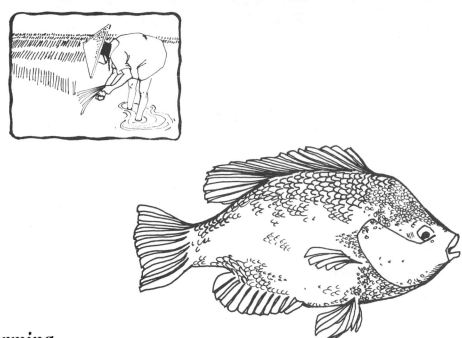

Fish Farming

Java is one of the most crowded countries in the world. In order to feed its people, Java needs to farm as much of its land as it can.

As in most countries in Asia, rice is the most important food in Java. People grow rice on most of the country's land. But the people need to eat other kinds of foods, too. In Java, farmers also raise another crop on their rice farms. Java farmers grow fish.

The farmers "plant" fish with their rice, which must grow in water. Into their flooded rice fields, the farmers put small fish called tilapia (tə lä'-pē ə). The tilapia looks something like the American sunfish. It grows very quickly. In only two weeks, tilapia eggs hatch and change into young fish.

The growing tilapia swim and feed among the rice plants. Because they eat young mosquitoes, they help keep down diseases caused by the insects.

When the rice is about to become ripe, the fields are drained. The fish have grown for three months. Now six to eight inches long, they are big enough to eat.

Fish add protein to the diet of those who eat them. In some countries, people still do not get enough protein to be healthy. But the farmers in Java have found an easy way to grow good food.

1. The most important food in many countries in Asia is
   a. bread.   c. rice.
   b. fruit.   d. meat.

2. The word in paragraph 5 that means *ready to harvest* is

   _____ .

3. The words "one of the most crowded countries in the world" in the

   first paragraph describe _____ .

4. The story does not say so, but it makes you think that
   a. the people of Java have nothing to eat.
   b. not all kinds of fish would grow in rice fields.
   c. tilapia are grown for food all over the world.

5. The tilapia is a fish that
   a. grows very quickly.
   b. eats rice plants.
   c. lives only two weeks.

6. The farmers of Java grow tilapia to add protein to their diets.
   Yes   No   Does not say

7. On the whole, this story is about
   a. Asian countries.
   b. young mosquitoes.
   c. growing tilapia.

8. Why does Java need to farm as much of its land as it can?
   a. Java has many people to feed.
   b. Java sells much food to other countries.
   c. People in Java cannot catch many fish.

9. Which statement does the story lead you to believe?
   a. Rice has much protein in it.
   b. Protein is a necessary part of the diet.
   c. People in Java do not like to eat tilapia.

Above the Frozen Layer

There are still places in the world that need settlers. One of these places is Alaska, our largest state. Settlers are important if Alaska is to become a strong and growing state.

People can become pioneers in Alaska for very little money. To aid settlers, the government will give each pioneer as much as 160 acres of land free. Settlers can build a log cabin from their own trees. But to make a living from the land takes hard work.

Because Alaska is so far north, its crops have a short growing season. Only a few weeks separate the frosts of spring and fall. Corn, tomatoes, apples, and peaches need more time to become ripe. Another problem for the settler is that much of Alaska has a layer of soil under the ground that is always frozen. This layer is called permafrost.

However, during June and July, the sun shines both night and day, and some crops grow rapidly. Cabbages weigh as much as 45 pounds. Beets, lettuce, strawberries, and potatoes are other crops that do well. Alaska grows some of the world's finest vegetables.

For those willing to work hard, Alaska offers a chance for a rewarding life.

FIND THE ANSWERS

1. The government will give pioneers in Alaska
   - a. clothing.
   - b. lumber.
   - c. seeds and plants.
   - d. free land.

2. The word in paragraph 2 that means *early settlers* is _____.

3. The words "a layer of soil under the ground that is always frozen" in paragraph 3 describe _____.

4. The story does not say so, but it makes you think that
   - a. Alaska is mostly farmland and forests.
   - b. Alaska has too many cities.
   - c. the sun shines both night and day all year in Alaska.

5. The state of Alaska lies
   - a. near South America.
   - b. in the far north.
   - c. in the middle of the United States.

6. Carrots and peanuts are crops that do well in Alaska.
   Yes   No   Does not say

7. On the whole, this story is about
   - a. growing crops in Alaska.
   - b. the government of the United States.
   - c. building a log cabin in the woods.

8. Why does the government give free land to pioneers in Alaska?
   - a. Alaska has so much land that it cannot all be sold.
   - b. With free land, settlers in Alaska do not have to work.
   - c. Free land helps new settlers to come and live in Alaska.

9. Which statement does the story lead you to believe?
   - a. Permafrost is needed to grow extra-large vegetables.
   - b. Crops with long growing seasons cannot grow in Alaska.
   - c. The sun shines all night during the late fall.

A New Tree for Ghana

Tete Kwashi (tet′tə kwä′shē) planted the first cacao trees in Ghana (gä′nə) in 1879. A blacksmith and a farmer, he had once worked on an island off the coast of Africa. He had seen the short, stubby cacao trees growing there. He knew that the beans that formed inside football-sized pods on their trunks were worth money. From those cacao beans came cocoa, and the trees were sometimes called "chocolate trees."

When he returned to his farm in Ghana, Tete Kwashi took a few seeds with him. He planted them and watched over the young trees carefully. A few years later, he harvested his first crop of cacao beans. He was able to sell the beans for a good price. Soon all his neighbors were planting cacao trees.

Tete Kwashi had found a crop that was just right for southern Ghana. The farmers had only small clearings in the tropical forest. The cacao tree grows best where it is sheltered by taller trees. The rich soil and warm, rainy weather were right for the cacao tree.

Today, the cacao trees of Ghana produce about one-third of all the world's chocolate. These trees may help Ghana become one of the most prosperous of Africa's new countries.

Tete Kwashi died many years ago. But on Ghana's coat of arms appears a picture of the important tree he brought home to his country.

1. Tete Kwashi was a
   a. doctor.   c. farmer.
   b. teacher.   d. lawyer.

2. The word in the first paragraph that means *short and thick* is

   _____.

3. The words "the important tree he brought home" in the last paragraph

   refer to the _____ _____.

4. The story does not say so, but it makes you think that
   a. some plants grow very well in new places.
   b. the cacao tree has always grown in Ghana.
   c. there are too many cacao trees in Ghana.

5. The cacao tree grows best in
   a. the desert.
   b. cold weather.
   c. rich soil.

6. Ghana is now the most prosperous African country.
   Yes   No   Does not say

7. On the whole, this story is about
   a. making chocolate.
   b. Ghana's cacao trees.
   c. warm, rainy weather.

8. Why did Tete Kwashi bring cacao seeds to Ghana?
   a. He knew cacao bean crops would be worth money.
   b. He wanted to make chocolate from the cacao beans.
   c. He wanted to show his neighbors what he had found.

9. Which statement does the story lead you to believe?
   a. Ghana grows nothing but cacao trees.
   b. Tete Kwashi did not want his neighbors to plant cacao seeds.
   c. Cacao beans are one of Ghana's most important products.

The Wonderful Gift

About 700,000 years ago, the world's weather turned colder. Great sheets of ice moved down and covered the Northern Hemisphere. The earth entered the Ice Age. During the Ice Age, many kinds of animals died out. Yet early humans were able to survive.

To survive, these people needed fire. They needed it to warm and light their caves, to cook their food, and to make their tools. They needed it to hunt. Sometimes hunters even lit fires to drive a herd of animals over a cliff to their death.

It was not easy for early humans to get fire. At first, they had to be very brave. When lightning or a volcano started a forest fire, they picked up a burning stick and carried it back to their caves. To keep the fire alive, they fed it dry sticks and leaves. They took their fire with them when they moved. They held a flaming torch or carried hot coals in an animal horn.

After many thousands of years, early humans learned to make fire. By hitting hard stones together, they could strike a light. Sometimes they rubbed wood against wood to start a fire by friction.

Humans are the only animals who have ever been able to use fire. For people, fire is nature's wonderful gift.

FIND THE ANSWERS

1. To live through the Ice Age, early humans needed
   - a. houses.
   - b. tools.
   - c. clothing.
   - d. fire.

2. The word in the first paragraph that means *to stay alive* is

   _____.

3. The words "the only animals who have ever been able to use fire" in

   the last paragraph refer to _____.

4. The story does not say so, but it makes you think that
   - a. there was no fire during the Ice Age.
   - b. fire was important to early people.
   - c. it was very easy for early people to get fire.

5. The first fires were started by
   - a. dry sticks and leaves.
   - b. lightning or volcanoes.
   - c. clever monkeys.

6. It took a long time for early people to learn to make their own fire.
   Yes   No   Does not say

7. On the whole, this story is about
   - a. forest fires during the Ice Age.
   - b. early people's ways of hunting.
   - c. early people and their use of fire.

8. Why did early people take fire with them when they moved?
   - a. At first, they did not know how to make their own fire.
   - b. The fire helped them find their way at night.
   - c. They thought hot coals would protect them in the forests.

9. Which statement does the story lead you to believe?
   - a. People started the first fires.
   - b. The first fires were started by accident.
   - c. Many animals are able to use fire.

From Needles to Leather

During the Ice Age, early humans had to face blizzards and freezing weather. They needed to protect their bodies from the cold.

Early humans were hunters. To keep warm, they covered themselves with the skin of the animals they killed. As time went on, they learned to shape animal skins into clothes.

To make their clothes, early humans invented new tools. They used a sharp stone knife to skin animals and to cut the hides. With a stone tool called an awl, they made holes in the animal skins. Then they used strips of hide to lace the skins together. Most important, they invented a needle with an eye and began the art of sewing. Some needles were made from the leg bones of large birds. Others were made of ivory.

Clothes made from animal skins became stiff and hard. To make them soft, early humans soaked them in water and then beat them. In time, they learned to make skins softer by rubbing them with animal fats.

Later, people learned to preserve the animal skins. They soaked the skins in water that they had first placed in the bark from an oak or willow tree. In this way, they turned the hides into leather. Leather did not rot or wear out easily.

1. Early humans made holes in animals skins with
   a. their fingers.
   b. a piece of wood.
   c. their teeth.
   d. an awl.

2. The word in paragraph 3 that means *the bony material making up elephants' tusks* is _____.

3. The words "did not rot or wear out easily" in the last paragraph describe _____.

4. The story does not say so, but it makes you think that
   a. there were no trees during the Ice Age.
   b. early humans did not live through the Ice Age.
   c. early humans slept in their clothes.

5. During the Ice Age, early humans needed to protect themselves
   a. from fires caused by lightning.
   b. against freezing weather.
   c. from large birds.

6. Early humans made cloth to use in making clothing.
   Yes   No   Does not say

7. On the whole, this story is about
   a. people's need to wear clothing.
   b. the art of sewing.
   c. the bark from oak and willow trees.

8. Why did early humans soak animal skins in water and bark?
   a. They were getting ready to eat the animal skins.
   b. They were trying to wash their clothes.
   c. They wanted to preserve the skins.

9. Which statement does the story lead you to believe?
   a. Early humans had many tools.
   b. Sewing is a very old art.
   c. People still use an awl to make clothes.

Tools of Stone

In order to survive, early humans needed tools. They needed spears for hunting. They needed scraping and cutting tools to turn the dead animals into food and clothing. They needed tools with which to make other tools.

These people did not know how to use metal. They used a glasslike stone called flint to make tools. By hitting a piece of flint with another stone, early humans caused chips to break away from the flint. These chips had sharp edges. They could be used as spearheads or as tools to cut and scrape. The flint that was left after chipping had a sharp point. It could be used as a hand ax.

As time went on, people learned to break off more and better chips called blades. Then they learned to shape their blades. They pushed hard against the edges of the blade with a sharp piece of bone. In this way, early Native Americans made their knives and arrowheads.

Early humans kept improving their tools and making new ones. By 8000 B.C., they had many tools of stone, wood, bone, ivory, and antler. They had spears, axes, knives, needles with eyes, and even a kind of saw.

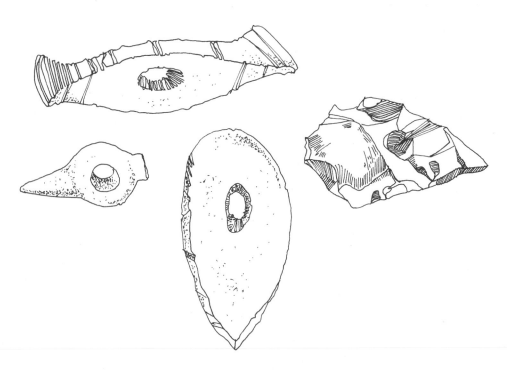

FIND THE ANSWERS

1. When they went hunting, early humans used
   a. metal.   c. axes.
   b. spears.   d. blades.

2. The word in the last paragraph that means *the horn of a deer* is

   _____.

3. The words "It could be used as a hand ax" in paragraph 2 describe

   the _____.

4. The story does not say so, but it makes you think that
   a. early humans did not hunt.
   b. early humans did not need tools.
   c. making tools was hard work.

5. Early humans used chips as
   a. tools and spearheads.
   b. food for their families.
   c. needles with eyes.

6. Early humans needed tools with sharp edges.
   Yes   No   Does not say

7. On the whole, this story is about
   a. the Native American.
   b. the clothing of early humans.
   c. the tools of early humans.

8. Why did early humans need tools that would cut and scrape?
   a. They used them to make houses.
   b. They used them to make clothing.
   c. They used them to fight with.

9. Which statement does the story lead you to believe?
   a. Even early humans had different tools.
   b. Early humans had only one kind of tool.
   c. The tools of early humans were made of metal.

They Burned Blubber

Do you wonder how the Eskimos were able to live in the Arctic? They needed special ways of getting their food, clothing, and housing. They needed special ways to travel.

Very few plants grow in the Arctic. To get food, the Eskimos hunted and fished. They hunted polar bears, seals, and whales. During certain seasons, they hunted reindeer and sea birds, and they fished for salmon.

In the winter, some Eskimos built igloos made of snow blocks. These snow houses protected them from the wind. To keep an igloo warm, they used a stone lamp. They burned blubber, the fat of sea animals, for fuel. In the summer, the Eskimos lived in tents made from animal skins.

The Eskimos needed clothes that were warm and kept out wind and water. They made their clothes from animal skins. Their high boots kept out the snow, and mittens protected their hands. Both men and women wore pants and a fur coat with a hood. An Eskimo woman had an extra-large coat so she could carry her baby on her back beneath it.

The Eskimos had to move about to hunt and fish and get the things they needed. In the winter, they traveled on a sled pulled by a team of dogs. In the summer, they traveled in a skin-covered canoe.

FIND THE ANSWERS

1. To get food, the Eskimos
   a. grew plants.
   b. raised animals.
   c. hunted and fished.
   d. went to the store.

2. The word in the first paragraph that means *the area near the North Pole* is _____.

3. The words "the fat of sea animals" in paragraph 3 describe

   _____.

4. The story does not say so, but it makes you think that Eskimos
   a. learned to live off the land.
   b. had no protection from the cold.
   c. live on green vegetables.

5. In winter, Eskimo women carried their babies
   a. in special kinds of skin-covered canoes.
   b. on their backs under extra-large coats.
   c. to watch the men hunting reindeer.

6. Eskimo women wear skirts made of animal skins.
   Yes   No   Does not say

7. On the whole, this story is about
   a. life among the Eskimos.
   b. fur coats with hoods.
   c. plants in the Arctic.

8. Why do Eskimos use high boots?
   a. Eskimos have very long legs.
   b. They are good fishing boots.
   c. High boots keep out the snow.

9. Which statement does the story lead you to believe?
   a. Eskimos travel in cars and buses.
   b. Eskimos are always on the move.
   c. Eskimos live in a warm, sunny land.

They Gave Their Country New Life

The small country of Israel (iz'-rē əl) is on the Mediterranean Sea. It is a young country that was formed by the United Nations in 1948. At that time, many new people were coming to Israel to live. The people of Israel needed to make their tiny land produce enough food for everyone. They needed to give their country new life.

Israel looked very different from the way it looks today. It was a land of sand dunes, swamps, and rocky hills. Most of the land could not be used for farming, and there was little water for irrigation. There were few industries.

The Israelis (iz rā'lēz) went to work. There were many things they had to do. They reclaimed many acres of land. Along the coast, they removed sand dunes and planted orchards of oranges and other citrus fruits. They drained swamps and planted fruit trees, vegetables, and other crops. Rock walls called terraces had once stood on the hills to keep the soil from washing away. These terraces were built again and trees planted.

The Israelis dug wells and built pipelines to carry water where it was needed. They built cities, towns, hospitals, and schools. They started new industries. Today, Israel is a land with new life.

FIND THE ANSWERS

1. To build their country, the Israelis had to
   a. build rocky hills.   c. reclaim acres of land.
   b. eat citrus fruits.   d. find the sand dunes.

2. The word in the first paragraph that means *grow* or *bring forth* is

   _____.

3. The words "looked very different" in paragraph 2 refer to

   _____.

4. The story does not say so, but it makes you think that
   a. sand dunes make very good farming land.
   b. the Israelis worked hard to change the land.
   c. there are too many pipelines carrying water.

5. Terraces on the hills once kept the soil from
   a. producing water.
   b. growing crops.
   c. washing away.

6. The Israelis had many things to do on the land.
   Yes   No   Does not say

7. On the whole, this story is about
   a. the age of the United Nations.
   b. the size of a small country.
   c. reclaiming the land of Israel.

8. Why did Israel need to produce so much food?
   a. Small countries need more food than big ones.
   b. People in Israel want to sell all their food.
   c. Many new people were going there to live.

9. Which statement does the story lead you to believe?
   a. Citrus fruits are an important crop in Israel.
   b. An orange is not a citrus fruit in Israel.
   c. It is not a good idea to reclaim land.

A Desert to Conquer

Mormons (môr′mənz) are people who belong to one of the many church groups in the United States. In 1846, thousands of Mormons had to leave their homes in Illinois because their neighbors did not like the Mormons' beliefs. The Mormons needed a place to live where no one would bother them. They went west to a new land.

The Mormons came to the Great Salt Lake Valley in what is now Utah. They were the first white settlers to choose to live there. Their new land was a desert covered with sagebrush and cactus. The only trees were in the mountains and near streams. The Mormons had to conquer the desert to make it grow the things they needed.

The Mormon settlers had the hard task of farming the desert. They dug miles of irrigation ditches to carry water from the streams into the dry soil. Once a piece of ground was watered, it was planted with crops.

The Mormon leaders sent groups of people to start new settlements. A group of settlers had much to do. They built forts to protect the people from Indians. They built houses of adobe or logs. They dug new irrigation ditches and farmed the land.

Life was very hard for the early Mormon settlers. Yet they conquered the desert because they did not give up.

FIND THE ANSWERS

1. The Great Salt Lake Valley is in
   a. Montana.   c. Utah.
   b. Nevada.   d. Idaho.

2. The word in paragraph 4 that means *sun-dried bricks* is

   _____.

3. The words "covered with sagebrush and cactus" in paragraph 2

   describe the _____.

4. The story does not say so, but it makes you think that
   a. the desert had to be watered by irrigation.
   b. farming in the desert is always very easy.
   c. sagebrush and cactus grow only on mountains.

5. The Mormons had to conquer the desert
   a. to keep their neighbors happy.
   b. to get up into the mountains.
   c. to grow the food they needed.

6. The Mormons were forced to leave Illinois.
   Yes   No   Does not say

7. On the whole, this story is about
   a. the Mormons in Utah.
   b. houses made of adobe.
   c. the first white settlers.

8. Why did the Mormons go west to a new land?
   a. They wanted to live with the Indians.
   b. They wanted to live where no one would bother them.
   c. They wanted to live where there was no salt.

9. Which statement does the story lead you to believe?
   a. Most deserts do not have very dry soil.
   b. All irrigation ditches are a mile long.
   c. It is not easy to move to a new land.

Windows in the Earth

Scientists want to know more about the inside of the earth. One way they find out about the earth's interior is by studying volcanoes.

Volcanoes are found in many parts of the world. They are deep cracks in the earth's crust. These cracks go far below the earth's surface and from them pour gases and hot, liquid rock called lava. Sometimes the ashes and lava coming out of the earth pile up around the crack. Then the volcano looks like a mountain.

There are different kinds of volcanoes. Some volcanoes throw gases and ashes high into the air. In other volcanoes, lava flows quietly out of the earth.

Scientists who study volcanoes have a dangerous job. They go to volcanoes to study the ashes, lava, and gases that come out. To protect their bodies from the heat and fire, they wear special suits.

Scientists must use special tools to study volcanoes. They keep records of the height and shape of volcanoes. They measure the temperature of red-hot lava. They measure the height of lava fountains that leap high in the air.

By studying volcanoes, scientists hope to learn what is happening even deeper below the earth's surface. For scientists, volcanoes are like windows in the earth's crust.

FIND THE ANSWERS

1. When they study volcanoes, scientists use
   - a. ashes and gases.
   - b. business suits.
   - c. red-hot lava.
   - d. special tools.

2. The word in the first paragraph that means *the inside of something* is _____.

3. The words "windows in the earth's crust" in the last paragraph refer to _____.

4. The story does not say so, but it makes you think that
   - a. it is hard to learn about the inside of the earth.
   - b. all scientists have safe, easy jobs.
   - c. scientists have never studied more than one volcano.

5. Some volcanoes throw out
   - a. water and ice.
   - b. gases and ashes.
   - c. dirt and sand.

6. Scientists study volcanoes at night.
   Yes   No   Does not say

7. On the whole, this story is about
   - a. studying volcanoes to learn about the earth.
   - b. scientists who protect their bodies.
   - c. volcanoes that look like windows.

8. Why do scientists need special tools?
   - a. Special tools help take measurements.
   - b. Special tools make windows in the volcanoes.
   - c. Special tools are used to measure the scientists.

9. Which statement does the story lead you to believe?
   - a. Volcanoes can be very dangerous.
   - b. All lava flows quietly out of the earth.
   - c. Scientists do not keep records.

Written in the Trees

How much rain has fallen on the earth in the past? People have not always kept weather records. Because scientists need a way to learn about past rainfall, they study tree rings.

A tree's trunk grows bigger each year. Beneath its bark, a tree adds a layer of new wood each year it lives. If you look at a tree stump, you can see the layers. They are called annual rings.

On some trees, all of the rings are the same width. But the ponderosa (pon də rō′sə) pines that grow in the American Southwest have rings of different widths. The soil in the Southwest is dry. The pines there depend on rainfall for water. In a year of good rainfall, they form wide rings. In a dry year, they form narrow ones.

Scientists do not have to cut down a pine to see its rings. With a special tool, they can remove a narrow piece of wood from the trunk without harming the tree. Then they look at the width of each ring to see how much rain fell in the year it formed.

Some pines are hundreds of years old and have hundreds of rings. These rings form an annual record of past rainfall in the Southwest.

FIND THE ANSWERS

1. The ponderosa pine grows in
   - a. the North.
   - b. the Southwest.
   - c. very wet places.
   - d. any soil.

2. The word in paragraph 2 that means *yearly* or *each year* is

   _____ .

3. The words "they form wide rings" in paragraph 3 refer to the

   _____ .

4. The story does not say so, but it makes you think that
   - a. a tree grows faster when it has a lot of water.
   - b. scientists cut down trees to study tree rings.
   - c. pine trees form wide rings every year.

5. A tree grows a new layer of wood
   - a. each week.
   - b. whenever it rains.
   - c. every year.

6. Scientists can remove wood from a tree without harming it.
   Yes   No   Does not say

7. On the whole, this story is about
   - a. why tree trunks grow bigger.
   - b. why scientists study tree rings.
   - c. trees that lived hundreds of years ago.

8. Why do scientists study the width of tree rings?
   - a. They want to know how big the tree will grow.
   - b. The rings tell them how much rain has fallen.
   - c. Scientists want to move the pine trees.

9. Which statement does the story lead you to believe?
   - a. Young trees have few annual rings.
   - b. The trunk of a tree never changes in size.
   - c. Trees in the Southwest do not need rain.

Clues to the Past

What kinds of animals lived on the earth millions of years ago? Scientists need a way to learn about those animals that lived in the past. For this reason, they study fossil animals that are preserved in the earth's crust.

Scientists have found many interesting fossils. Dinosaur eggs have been found that are over a million years old. Over the years, the eggs turned to stone. The footprints of some animals and the outlines of animal bodies have been found in rock. Bones and shells have been dug from the earth.

Fossils can tell scientists many things about an animal and its habits. The shape of a shell can tell how the animal moved. An animal's teeth can tell if it ate meat or grass.

Scientists make tests on the rock in which a fossil is found. They are able to learn how old the rock is. Then they know how long ago the animal lived.

Scientists compare fossil skeletons to the skeletons of living animals. This may help them to learn what kind of animal made the fossil.

Fossil animals might be called clues to the past. From fossils, scientists can tell where an animal lived, when it lived, and what it was like.

1. Scientists study fossils to learn about
    a. preserving the earth.   c. turning eggs to stone.
    b. animals of the past.   d. meat or grass.

2. The word in the first paragraph that means *kept safe* is

    _____.

3. The words "turned to stone" in paragraph 2 refer to the

    _____.

4. The story does not say so, but it makes you think that
    a. animals did not eat meat or grass long ago.
    b. it is not easy to tell what kind of animal made a fossil.
    c. scientists have been studying fossils for over a million years.

5. Scientists can tell what animals ate from studying
    a. their teeth.
    b. their eggs.
    c. the rocks.

6. Scientists have found many interesting fossils.
    Yes   No   Does not say

7. On the whole, this story is about
    a. scientists of the past.
    b. the study of fossil animals.
    c. looking for dinosaur eggs.

8. Why do scientists make tests on rocks that hold fossils?
    a. The tests may show how long ago the animals lived.
    b. The scientists want to know what the rocks are made of.
    c. Scientists want to know whether the rocks came from outer space.

9. Which statement does the story lead you to believe?
    a. Fossils cannot tell scientists anything important.
    b. Fossils can tell scientists the history of the earth.
    c. It is not a good idea to preserve the earth's crust.

A New Treaty

By 1961, the western part of Canada needed more electricity for its growing cities and industries. The United States needed protection from floods along the Columbia River.

The Columbia is a river that both countries share. It begins in Canada, high in the Rocky Mountains. It flows south into the United States before it empties into the Pacific Ocean.

Dams and power plants to make electricity were built on the lower part of the Columbia River in the United States. But the river's flow was not always the same. Storage dams high in the mountains could make the flow even. They could hold back water in spring and prevent floods. They could let the water flow again in autumn when it was needed.

The United States needed storage dams, but the best place to build them was in Canada. Canada needed electricity, but the best place to build power plants was in the United States.

The governments of the two countries signed a treaty. Canada agreed to build three large storage dams in the mountains. The United States agreed to build a new power plant and to make other plants larger. The new supply of electricity would be divided equally between the two countries. The river could then serve all the people better.

1. By 1961, the United States needed
   a. protection from Canada.   c. the western part of Canada.
   b. protection from floods.   d. a river to share with Canada.

2. The word in paragraph 3 that means *stop* is _____.

3. The words "a river that both countries share" in paragraph 2 describe

   the _____.

4. The story does not say so, but it makes you think that
   a. countries should not share their rivers.
   b. the Columbia River is owned by the United States.
   c. Canada and the United States are good neighbors.

5. The new supply of electricity was
   a. needed only by people living on the river.
   b. used only for the western part of Canada.
   c. divided equally between the countries.

6. The Columbia River flows through only one country.
   Yes   No   Does not say

7. On the whole, this story is about
   a. the wise use of a river.
   b. making power plants big.
   c. storage dams in mountains.

8. Why did the two countries sign a treaty?
   a. It helped them decide where to put the river.
   b. The people forced them to do this.
   c. They wanted to share the river.

9. Which statement does the story lead you to believe?
   a. The flow of a river is always the same.
   b. Two countries can solve problems by working together.
   c. The best place for storage dams is in the south.

The Road across the Mountains

The first thirteen states lay east of the Allegheny Mountains. Ohio, which wanted to become the fourteenth state, was west of the mountains.

The members of the United States Congress thought Ohio was too far away. If Ohio became a state, they said, it would need to be closer to the other states.

The one thing that could bring Ohio closer to the eastern states was a road. At that time, only steep, winding trails led over the mountains. A good road that wagons could use all year would make Ohio seem nearer. Travelers could cross the mountains faster, and mail could travel more quickly. But such a road would be hard to build. It would cost more money than Congress had for building roads.

Congress passed a law in 1802 that allowed Ohio to become a state. This law also provided a way to build the needed road. There was much empty land in Ohio that could be sold to settlers. As this land was sold, five cents of each dollar received was to be used to build roads.

The road across the mountains was started in 1811. In 1818, it stretched from Cumberland, Maryland, to the Ohio River. It was called the Cumberland Road. Today, it is a big highway called U.S. 40. You can find it on any road map.

FIND THE ANSWERS

1. Ohio wanted to become
   - a. part of the West.
   - b. part of Congress.
   - c. a city.
   - d. a state.

2. The word in paragraph 3 that means *rough paths* is _____.

3. The words "west of the mountains" in the first paragraph describe

   _____.

4. The story does not say so, but it makes you think that
   - a. there are laws against building hard roads.
   - b. roads help bring people closer together.
   - c. it is hard to find roads on a road map.

5. At one time, only steep, winding trails
   - a. were found in the East.
   - b. led over the mountains.
   - c. were good for wagons.

6. The Cumberland Road is still being used.
   Yes   No   Does not say

7. On the whole, this story is about
   - a. making Ohio part of western United States.
   - b. building a road from Cumberland, Maryland, to the Ohio River.
   - c. how Congress passes laws about the Ohio River.

8. Why did Ohio want a road across the mountains?
   - a. It would help people leave Congress.
   - b. It would help Ohio become a state.
   - c. It would keep the people in the East.

9. Which statement does the story lead you to believe?
   - a. Ohio became our fourteenth state.
   - b. There was no Congress long ago.
   - c. Steep, winding trails make the best roads.

New Schools for New Lands

Soon after the American Revolution, western land belonging to the United States was opened to settlers. Many people were eager to make new homes in the rich, empty land west of the Allegheny Mountains. They moved as families, taking their children with them. The children needed schools.

The members of the United States Congress believed that education was important. Every child needed to learn to read and write and understand his country's laws. But they knew it would not be easy for the settlers to start new schools. At first, there was not enough money to build buildings and pay teachers.

In 1785, Congress passed a law that helped the settlers pay for the schools they needed. The law set aside some of the new land for school purposes. All new land was divided into townships six miles square. Each township was divided into thirty-six sections, each one mile square. One section in every township was called the school section. All money gained from the sale or use of this land was used for schools.

School section land helped start schools all the way from the Allegheny Mountains to the Pacific Ocean. Later, Congress set aside larger areas of public land to help new states start the colleges and universities they needed.

FIND THE ANSWERS

1. The members of the United States Congress believed
    a. education was important.   c. there were too many schools.
    b. children needed to work.   d. children should not read.

2. The word in paragraph 3 that means *reasons* or *aims* is

    _____.

3. The words "eager to make new homes in the rich, empty land" in the

    first paragraph refer to the _____.

4. The story does not say so, but it makes you think that
    a. school was important to the settlers.
    b. it was easy to start the new schools.
    c. the children had to build the schools.

5. Townships are
    a. found only in the mountains.
    b. six miles square
    c. also called school sections.

6. All settlers paid the same amount for their land.
    Yes   No   Does not say

7. On the whole, this story is about
    a. understanding the laws of the country.
    b. helping settlers get schools started.
    c. dividing townships into square sections.

8. Why did the children need schools?
    a. They wanted members of Congress to be happy.
    b. They needed a building to raise money.
    c. They needed to learn to read and write.

9. Which statement does the story lead you to believe?
    a. The best schools are found near the ocean.
    b. Education is important for all the people.
    c. Too much land is needed for public schools.

Artists without Brushes

Children need ways to show what they think and feel. For this reason, many children enjoy finger painting. Using their fingers, they can paint their own pictures and make designs.

People started finger painting long ago. Early humans used their hands to paint animals on the walls of caves. Hundreds of years ago, Chinese artists used their fingers to draw with ink.

Modern finger painting was started by an American school teacher named Ruth Shaw. A child in her class hurt a finger. The teacher told the student to put some iodine on the cut. Later, she found the child using the iodine and all ten fingers to draw designs.

From this, she got the idea of letting children rub paint on paper with their fingers.

To finger paint, children use a special paint and paper. The paint must be harmless to the skin and wash off easily. The paper has a shiny coating on one side that holds the paint.

The young artists wet the paper before they begin their work. They paint standing up so they will have more room to move their arms. They can paint with their fingers or with their elbows, arms, or hands. As they slide the paint over the paper, they turn a sea of color into a bright design.

FIND THE ANSWERS

1. In China, artists used their fingers to
   - a. draw standing up.
   - b. draw with ink.
   - c. make colors in the sea.
   - d. paint their teacher.

2. The word in paragraph 3 that means *a medicine that is put on cuts* is _____.

3. The words "a shiny coating on one side" in paragraph 4 describe the _____.

4. The story does not say so, but it makes you think that
   - a. only children with hurt fingers can draw.
   - b. finger painting can be a lot of fun.
   - c. only children like to use finger paint.

5. Finger paints must be
   - a. made from iodine.
   - b. hard to wash off.
   - c. harmless to the skin.

6. Finger painting is only good for making designs.
   Yes   No   Does not say

7. On the whole, this story is about
   - a. American school teachers.
   - b. Chinese artists who painted on walls.
   - c. a new way to paint.

8. Why does one side of the paper have a shiny coating?
   - a. It holds the paint.
   - b. It makes the paint sticky.
   - c. It makes the paint slide off.

9. Which statement does the story lead you to believe?
   - a. Finger painting is not a new idea.
   - b. You must be Chinese to use finger paints.
   - c. It is not good to use special paints.

Some Work with Metal

Some artists make figures from stone, clay, or other materials. These figures may be shaped like a human being or an animal. Sometimes they are shaped like nothing found in nature. We call all these works sculpture.

The artist who makes a sculpture needs to know how to use certain materials and tools. A figure may be carved from a piece of wood or shaped from clay.

In the past, sculpture was usually made from stone, wood, bone, or ivory. But today artists are using new materials. Many sculptures are now made from metal.

Many artists find metal a good material to use. Using metal, artists can make their sculptures almost any size they wish. A metal sculpture can look light and airy, but the metal itself is very strong. Artists can use metal in different ways.

Some artists make sculptures by joining together pieces of metal. These pieces may be different sizes and shapes. A sculptor uses a special kind of torch to weld the pieces together. As artists work, they must wear special clothes, gloves, and face coverings to protect themselves from the heat.

Perhaps you will visit an art museum soon. You may see some very exciting and interesting sculptures made with metal.

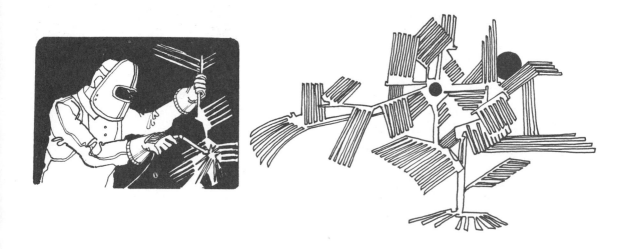

1. A metal sculpture is usually
   a. heavy and weak.
   b. shaped like an animal.
   c. strong.
   d. small.

2. The word in paragraph 5 that means *to heat and join metal* is

   _____ .

3. The words "almost any size" in paragraph 4 describe

   _____ .

4. The story does not say so, but it makes you think that
   a. it is hard to make metal sculpture.
   b. all artists work with metal.
   c. a torch is a special kind of brush.

5. Pieces of a metal sculpture can be
   a. welded together.
   b. pasted together.
   c. taken apart easily.

6. All sculptures are the same size.
   Yes   No   Does not say

7. On the whole, this story is about
   a. a different kind of painting.
   b. a new way to make sculpture.
   c. a new kind of face covering.

8. Why do some artists like to work with metal?
   a. Metal lasts longer than stone or clay.
   b. The artists can use metal in different ways.
   c. The artists cannot buy other materials today.

9. Which statement does the story lead you to believe?
   a. A sculpture in metal is shaped like a human being.
   b. Artists who work with stone wear special clothes.
   c. The materials artists use can change.

A Way to Decorate a Building

People need ways to decorate their buildings. Some artists use mosaics to help make buildings beautiful.

A mosaic is a picture made from bits and pieces of glass. Shells, small stones, tiles, and other hard and interesting materials can also be used. The surface of a good mosaic reflects light. The materials used in the mosaic work together to form a very colorful picture.

Mosaic art began in Egypt over 5,000 years ago and then spread around the world. At first, mosaics were used to cover floors. As time went on, they were used to decorate the inside walls of large and beautiful churches. Mosaics were often used on the outside surfaces of buildings. They did not wear away in the sun and the rain.

Mosaic art can also make modern buildings more beautiful and interesting. In Mexico, the library building at the National University of Mexico has a mosaic around its top ten stories. The mosaic covers the four sides of the building and measures over an acre of art.

Juan O'Gorman (won ō gôr′mən) helped to plan the building. The mosaic was made with building materials from every Mexican state. The mosaic tells a story about Mexico's past and present. The bright patterns can be seen from far away.

106

FIND THE ANSWERS

1. Mosaic art began over 5,000 years ago in
   - a. Mexico.
   - c. England.
   - b. Italy.
   - d. Egypt.

2. The word in the last paragraph that means *designs* is _____.

3. The words "a picture made from bits and pieces of glass" in paragraph 2 describe _____.

4. The story does not say so, but it makes you think that
   - a. mosaics are used only for floors.
   - b. many things can be used in mosaics.
   - c. only Juan O'Gorman can make mosaics.

5. The library building in Mexico has mosaics made
   - a. with paintings from every state in the United States.
   - b. with materials from every Mexican state.
   - c. from the flags of every state in Mexico.

6. Some buildings in our country are decorated with mosaics.
   Yes   No   Does not say

7. On the whole, this story is about
   - a. the National University.
   - b. the art of mosaics.
   - c. making buildings modern.

8. Why were mosaics often used on the outside surfaces of buildings?
   - a. They cost less than other materials.
   - b. They did not wear away in the sun and rain.
   - c. They were easy to put on buildings.

9. Which statement does the story lead you to believe?
   - a. Mosaics are all one color.
   - b. Mosaics last a long time.
   - c. Mosaic art began in Mexico.

The Clever Old Woman
of Carcassonne

Once, long ago, the whole town of Carcassonne was in siege. Outside the town gates waited a large army of enemies.

The people of the town were afraid to go outside their gates in order to get more meal to eat. If they did go outside, they would be killed by their enemies.

Hunger and sickness had killed many people. Those who were still alive were hungry and unhappy.

The mayor of the town called all the people to a meeting. "My friends," he said, "we shall have to give ourselves up to the enemy. All our provisions are gone."

Suddenly a little old woman came forward. Her clothes were worn and torn. She said in a loud voice, "Don't give up yet! I am sure the enemy will soon go away. Do as I tell you, and the town will be saved."

The mayor said, "All right, Old Woman, tell us your plan."

The old woman said, "Bring me a cow."

"A cow!" cried the mayor, "there is not one cow left in the whole town. Our cows were eaten long ago."

The old woman repeated, "I must have a cow! Bring me a cow!"

The people looked everywhere for a cow. They looked in every yard.

At last the mayor found a cow in the house of an old miser. He had hidden the animal, hoping to sell her for a large amount of money.

The mayor took the cow from the miser. He and the people led the cow to the old woman.

"Now," ordered the old woman, "bring me a bushel of meal."

"Old Woman, there is no meal left in our town," the mayor said sadly.

The clever old woman said that without a bushel of meal she could not save the town. Then the people searched every house in the town. Somehow they gathered a few grains here and a few grains there. At last they had a full bushel of meal.

"Now bring me some water," said the old woman. This they did with no trouble.

The old woman watered the meal to make it heavier. Then she fed the meal to the cow.

"It is wicked to feed good grain to the cow when our children are hungry!" cried the mayor.

The old woman smiled and only shook her head.

Night had fallen before the cow had finished eating. The old woman led the cow to the town gates.

"Open the gates," she ordered the guard. The big iron doors swung open, and the old woman quickly pushed the cow through them.

The enemy soldiers heard the squeaking of the doors. The soldiers

ran to the gate. They were glad to find the cow and quickly drove her to their camp.

"Where did you find this cow?" asked the enemy king.

"Just outside the gates of the town,"

said the enemy soldiers. "The Carcassonne people must have let her out to graze."

"Oh," said the king, "I thought they were starving in there! But I must be wrong, for if they were hungry, they would have eaten this cow."

"Yes, they must have more provisions than we thought they had," said the enemy soldiers.

"It has been a long time since *we* ate fresh meat," said their king. "Kill the cow, and we shall have steak for dinner!"

Quickly the soldiers killed the cow. They cut the cow open and were astonished to find her stomach filled with grain.

The soldiers ran to tell the king, "There is grain in the stomach of the cow!"

The king answered, "The people of Carcassonne must have a large provision of grain. They have so much grain that they feed it to their animals. This means we shall have to wait here too long before they surrender. And we ourselves will probably starve before they surrender."

And so the king gave orders to break up camp. The enemy king and his army went away that very night.

And that was how the town of Carcassonne became free again. The grateful people carried the old woman on their shoulders through the streets.

The mayor gave her a fat purse filled with money. With this reward the smart old woman married the miser, and they lived in comfort for the rest of their lives.

708 words

110

III

The Success of a Community Depends on Cooperation Among Its Members

In this section you will read about how the success of a community depends on cooperation among its members. You will read about these things from the standpoint of space, history, biology, economics, anthropology, geography, earth science, political science, and art.

Keep these questions in mind when you are reading.

1. What makes a successful community?

2. Does the individual need to give to a community, or only to use it?

3. What are some ways that people work together to make a better community?

4. Do all of us have something that can help a community?

5. How do communities help individuals?

A Lark in the Sky

Until 1957 the only satellite in the sky was the moon. Today, over 200 small, mechanical moons are in orbit around the earth. Some of the satellites still radio back facts about weather and space. Others have stopped broadcasting and orbit in silence.

One satellite sent broadcasts for ten years. Its name is *Alouette* (ä lü et′), a French word that means "lark." *Alouette* was special in another way, too. It was the first satellite in orbit that was not built by the United States or Russia. Even though its name is French, *Alouette* was built in Canada.

Canada wanted to learn more about the upper air and radio noise from space. Canada's engineers could build satellites, but they had no way to put them into orbit. So the United States and Canada decided to work together. Canada built the satellite. Our country built a rocket to send the satellite into space.

Alouette was launched from California on September 29, 1962. It proved to be one of the best satellites ever built.

Soon after *Alouette* was launched, Canada and the United States set up plans to work on other satellites. By working together, the two countries could do much more than could either country alone.

1. *Alouette* is a French word that means
   a. "satellite."   c. "lady."
   b. "orbit."   d. "lark."

2. The word in the last paragraph that means *sent into space* is

   _____.

3. The words "Small, mechanical moons" in the first paragraph describe

   _____.

4. The story does not say so, but it makes you think that
   a. Canada and the United States do not work well together.
   b. *Alouette* was built to look like a bird.
   c. Canada and the United States are good neighbors.

5. *Alouette* was built in
   a. the United States.
   b. Canada.
   c. France.

6. All satellites are made by people.
   Yes   No   Does not say

7. On the whole, this story is about
   a. a satellite launched by people from two countries.
   b. rockets that send satellites up into space.
   c. how the names of satellites are chosen.

8. Why did the United States and Canada build *Alouette* together?
   a. They could build a much bigger satellite together.
   b. Neither country had enough money to build it alone.
   c. They could do more together than alone.

9. Which statement does the story lead you to believe?
   a. The moon is now the only satellite in the sky.
   b. The first mechanical satellite was launched in 1957.
   c. *Alouette* was built by French engineers.

Flight of the Friendship 7

One night in February 1962, John H. Glenn, Jr., flew over Australia. The man in the Mercury capsule was alone, but friendly voices reached him by radio. On the dark land 100 miles below, he saw a sprinkling of lights. They marked the city of Perth, where people had turned on their lights as a greeting to him.

In *Friendship 7*, Glenn radioed, "The lights show up very well. Thank everybody for turning them on." His capsule raced on to the east.

During his three orbits of the earth, Glenn could always reach one of eighteen tracking stations. Some of them were on ships at sea. Others were in the United States.

Many of the stations had been built with the help of other countries. These countries allowed Americans to bring in radio equipment and set it up. Without the help of such lands as Nigeria, Zanzibar, and Mexico, there would have been breaks in the worldwide radio network.

John Glenn, Jr., was the first American to orbit the earth. For his flight, the tracking network covered 60,000 route miles. Five hundred people worked in the stations along the route. Since his flight, the network has grown. Today, it covers more than 100,000 route miles and has about one hundred stations. One-third of these stations are outside the United States.

1. During his flights, John H. Glenn, Jr., could always reach a
    a. ship at sea. c. lighted city.
    b. tracking station. d. space capsule.

2. The word in paragraph 4 that means *a number of tracking stations* is

    _____ .

3. The words "Nigeria, Zanzibar, and Mexico" in paragraph 4 refer to

    _____ .

4. The story does not say so, but it makes you think that
    a. *Friendship 7* stopped in Perth, Australia.
    b. all tracking stations are inside the United States.
    c. radio equipment is important in space flights.

5. John H. Glenn, Jr., was the first American to
    a. radio a town in Australia.
    b. orbit the earth.
    c. build a tracking station.

6. Some tracking stations are in other countries.
    Yes   No   Does not say

7. On the whole, this story is about
    a. talking to ships at sea around the world.
    b. breaks in the worldwide radio network.
    c. the first American orbit of the earth.

8. Why did the people in Perth turn on their lights?
    a. They wanted to greet John Glenn.
    b. It was time for them to get up.
    c. They wanted to see the *Friendship 7*.

9. Which statement does the story lead you to believe?
    a. Nigeria, Zanzibar, and Mexico turned on their lights.
    b. Countries must work together to track satellites.
    c. John Glenn, Jr., is the only American to orbit the earth.

News from Venus

Venus is our nearest neighbor in space. Like the earth, Venus is a planet that spins around the sun. As yet, no one from our planet has visited Venus.

But on October 18, 1967, a Russian spacecraft reached the surface of Venus. The spacecraft's name was *Venus 4*. When it neared the planet, it dropped a small space station. Fifteen miles above the surface, the station began to broadcast information.

However, the information was not picked up in Russia. Before the flight, the Russians asked scientists in England to help track their spacecraft. The English scientists used radio telescopes in their work. They also picked up radio signals sent by *Venus 4*.

Thirty-five hours after the Russian spacecraft landed on Venus, our *Mariner V* spacecraft flew by. It also sent back radio signals. This information was added to that received from *Venus 4*.

The scientists learned many new facts from *Venus 4*. They learned that the clouds on Venus are as hot as 536° F. The clouds are made up of dust and very little water.

The United States, Russia, and England had worked together to learn more about Venus. They made it possible for all countries to find out new things about our neighbor in space.

FIND THE ANSWERS

1. *Venus 4* was a
   a. small space station.
   b. Russian spacecraft.
   c. neighbor in space.
   d. United States spacecraft.

2. The word in paragraph 4 that means *signs that give information* is

   _____.

3. The words "as hot as 536° F." in paragraph 5 describe the

   _____.

4. The story does not say so, but it makes you think that
   a. we now know much more about the surface of Venus.
   b. the Russians were the first to land a human on Venus.
   c. the English asked the Russians to track *Mariner V.*

5. The Russians asked scientists in England to
   a. broadcast information to *Venus 4.*
   b. help find the spacecraft *Mariner V.*
   c. help track their satellite.

6. The clouds on Venus have very little water.
   Yes   No   Does not say

7. On the whole, this story is about
   a. *Mariner V* landing on Venus.
   b. sending a spacecraft to Venus.
   c. English scientists in spacecraft.

8. Why were *Venus 4* and *Mariner V* sent into space?
   a. Russia and the United States were having a race.
   b. They carried humans to the planet Venus.
   c. Scientists wanted to know more about Venus.

9. Which statement does the story lead you to believe?
   a. Sharing information helps everyone.
   b. Russia always works alone.
   c. American scientists helped track *Venus 4.*

From Votes to Notes

Not long ago American women were not allowed to vote. They were not supposed to work away from their homes. This way of life bothered many women, and so they did something about it.

First, women started what was called the suffrage movement. They worked hard for their right to vote. They made speeches and talked to people. Getting others to listen was not easy. These women who fought for their right to vote were called suffragettes. One famous suffragette was Susan B. Anthony.

After they won the vote, women decided to do more with their lives. At first they became nurses and school teachers. Slowly they began to work in offices. During World War II, women became riveters. Now some women drive trucks and buses.

In 1955 Marian Anderson became the first black singer at the Metropolitan Opera in New York City. In 1976 Maestro Sarah Caldwell became the first woman to lead the Metropolitan orchestra. These women of note really knew their notes!

The first woman ever elected to the United States Congress was Jeannette Rankin. She served from 1917 to 1919.

The first black woman to become a member of Congress was Shirley Chisholm.

Women are becoming doctors, race horse jockeys, and even auctioneers.

Do you suppose that when a woman is President, she will be called "the Mother of our Country"? If this President has a husband, would he be known as the "First Gentleman"?

1. American women wanted to
    a. go out once a week.
    b. win the vote and find new kinds of work.
    c. do the same kind of work always.
    d. sleep late every day.

2. The word in paragraph 4 that means *belonging to a large city* is

    _____ .

3. The words, "These women who fought for their right to vote" in paragraph 2 describe the _____ .

4. The story does not say so, but it makes you think that
    a. Susan B. Anthony was a riveter.
    b. Marian Anderson studied music many years.
    c. Sarah Caldwell likes to sew.

5. Today women
    a. drive trucks and buses.
    b. never stay home.
    c. seldom vote.
    d. cannot be in Congress.

6. American women can be members of Congress.
    Yes   No   Does not say

7. On the whole, the story makes you think that
    a. women cannot conduct an orchestra.
    b. only men sing at the Metropolitan Opera.
    c. women did something about their way of life.

8. Why did women become riveters during World War II?
    a. They had nothing else to do.
    b. The men were away fighting.
    c. Riveting was a fun thing to do.

9. Which statement does the story lead you to believe?
    a. A woman will never be President.
    b. Women in the future will hold more kinds of jobs.
    c. Auctioneers cannot vote.

Husking the Corn

In Colonial days, farm families worked from sunrise to sunset and sometimes longer. People had little time for play. They did not have a chance to see other people as much as we do today. But sometimes they were able to turn hard work into good times and still visit with their neighbors.

In Virginia, Indian corn was an important crop. In late autumn after the weather had turned cold, the corn was ready to be harvested. Each ear had a cover of leaves called the husk. The colonists pulled ears of corn from the dry stalks and stored the ears of corn. Later, they held a corn-husking party.

On a clear night in November, neighboring families gathered to husk the corn. They lit lanterns in a barn and piled the corn in high mounds on the floor. Then everyone went to work.

Most of the corn was yellow or white. But from time to time, a red ear was found. The person who found it was supposed to have good luck.

As people worked together, they enjoyed each other's company. There was cider to drink and cakes and cookies to eat. Corn huskings were a favorite with boys and girls because they liked the chance to have a party.

FIND THE ANSWERS

1. An important crop in Virginia was
   - a. cider.
   - b. red corn.
   - c. cakes and cookies.
   - d. Indian corn.

2. The word in paragraph 3 that means *piles* or *heaps* is _____.

3. The words "a cover of leaves" in paragraph 2 describe the

   _____.

4. The story does not say so, but it makes you think that
   - a. after husking corn, the colonists ate dinner.
   - b. the colonists had to husk corn in the dark.
   - c. corn had to be husked before it could be used.

5. Corn-husking parties were held in
   - a. houses from sunrise to sunset.
   - b. the fields at noon.
   - c. barns at night.

6. Corn husking took place in the spring.

   Yes   No   Does not say

7. On the whole, this story is about
   - a. harvesting an important crop.
   - b. Indians during Colonial days.
   - c. dances held in colonial barns.

8. Why did boys and girls like corn huskings?
   - a. They liked the chance to dress up.
   - b. They liked to count the ears of corn.
   - c. They liked to have parties.

9. Which statement does the story lead you to believe?
   - a. Most of the ears of corn husked were red.
   - b. The colonists knew how to mix fun with work.
   - c. All the people who husked corn had good luck.

Working Together Was Fun

After the East Coast of America became thickly settled, pioneers moved west into the wilderness. These pioneers faced the same hard tasks as had America's first settlers. Like the early settlers, the pioneers were able to finish many of these jobs by working together.

Pioneers in Indiana found the land covered by thick forests. When pioneers wanted land for farming, they cut down the trees themselves. Neighbors were asked to help the pioneers pile the logs into heaps.

On the day set, people arrived early in the morning. About fifty people usually came. The children played while the grown-ups did the work.

There was much work to be done. A large dinner was cooked. People formed teams to lift and carry the logs into piles. Hard work was turned into fun. Each team tried to beat the other by stacking a larger pile. Water was carried to the people doing the work.

Finally the work was done. The stacked logs could be used for new buildings or for winter firewood. But it was not all work. They played games and ran races. A big dinner ended a hard but happy day of working together.

FIND THE ANSWERS

1. Indiana pioneers found the land covered by
   a. grassy plains.   c. the ocean.
   b. thick forests.   d. a vast desert.

2. The word in the first paragraph that means *a forest area with no people*

   in it is _____.

3. The words "tried to beat the other" in paragraph 4 refer to each

   _____.

4. The story does not say so, but it makes you think that
   a. stacking logs into piles took only a few minutes.
   b. pioneers cut trees into logs by themselves.
   c. groups of people worked together to cut down trees.

5. Teams of people lifted and carried
   a. wood to build a house.
   b. food to the tables.
   c. the logs into piles.

6. The stacked logs were always used to build fences.
   Yes   No   Does not say.

7. On the whole, this story is about
   a. planting corn in the Indiana wilderness.
   b. working together to stack logs.
   c. pioneer games and races after dinner.

8. Why did the pioneers cut down their trees?
   a. They wanted to clear the land for farming.
   b. They were making roads to the west.
   c. They did not like to live in thick forests.

9. Which statement does the story lead you to believe?
   a. Children worked together to stack logs.
   b. Pioneer children did not get to play.
   c. Pioneer families did not see each other every day.

Beavers Share the Work

A beaver colony may have one beaver family, or it may have three or four. Across a stream, beavers build a dam of sticks, stones, and mud. In the pond that forms behind the dam, beavers build the lodge in which they live. It is made of earth and sticks.

The beavers in the colony work together. They must check their dam every day except in winter. They fix it if it leaks. Sometimes the beavers have to repair their lodge or make it larger.

Beavers work hard to get their food. They cut down trees with their sharp teeth and eat the bark and branches. In the fall, they gather and store a supply of food in the lodge. They will need this food in the winter.

With so much work to do, all beavers in the colony must do their share. Even the young beavers do what they can. They help work on the dam and the lodge. They cut down the small, young trees.

If the beavers must move a heavy log, a pair of animals works together. They put their heads or bodies against the log and push.

When winter comes, the beavers' pond freezes over. The beavers are safe inside their lodge. Because they worked together, they have food enough to last them until spring.

FIND THE ANSWERS

1. Except for the winter months, beavers check their dams
   a. each fall.
   b. every day.
   c. in the spring.
   d. each week.

2. The word in the first paragraph that means *a group of beavers living together* is _____.

3. The words "They fix it if it leaks" in paragraph 2 refer to the

   _____.

4. The story does not say so, but it makes you think that
   a. beavers are lazy animals.
   b. beavers do not come out in winter.
   c. beavers look for food during the winter.

5. Pond beavers make their lodges of
   a. pieces of food.
   b. earth and sticks.
   c. bark and tree trunks.

6. Young beavers help with the work.
   Yes   No   Does not say

7. On the whole, this story is about
   a. sharing the work in a beaver colony.
   b. animals that live in the woods.
   c. how beavers are able to cut down trees.

8. Why do beavers gather and store food in the fall?
   a. They like the fall weather.
   b. They want to sleep all winter.
   c. They will need food in the winter.

9. Which statement does the story lead you to believe?
   a. Beavers cannot move heavy logs.
   b. Each beaver has some kind of work to do.
   c. Beavers eat nothing at all during the winter.

Together in the Cold

Antarctica (ant ärk′təkə) is the continent that stretches around the South Pole. During its winter, Antarctica is the coldest place on earth. The temperature may go down to 80 degrees below zero. Winds may reach 100 miles an hour.

Every fall, thousands of emperor penguins come to Antarctica. They return from the ocean where they have spent the summer. They gather on the desert of snow and ice that is their winter home.

The emperors are almost four feet tall and are the largest of all penguins. They come to Antarctica to lay their eggs, hatch them, and raise their young. By living together, they can help each other in several ways.

The emperors help keep each other warm at night. They stand close together in large oval-shaped groups called turtles. Those penguins on the outside of a turtle stand with their backs to the cold. Those inside the turtle crowd together. The penguins change places from time to time and give those on the outside a chance to get warm.

The emperors also help each other care for the young birds. When a baby penguin is old enough, it joins the other youngsters in penguin nur-series. They stay close together. A few adult baby-sitters watch them. With their young well cared for, the other penguins are free to fish miles away.

1. Emperor penguins live in the land around
    a. North America.   c. the South Pole.
    b. the United States.   d. the North Pole.

2. The word in the last paragraph that means *grown-up* is

   _____.

3. The words "stand with their backs to the cold" in paragraph 4 describe

   the _____.

4. The story does not say so, but it makes you think that
    a. emperor penguins do not care for their young.
    b. penguins can live in very cold weather.
    c. emperor penguins eat turtles.

5. Emperor penguins come to Antarctica to
    a. lay their eggs.
    b. escape from humans.
    c. try to keep warm.

6. Adult emperor penguins are about one foot tall.
    Yes   No   Does not say

7. On the whole, this story is about
    a. nurseries for children.
    b. how emperor penguins live.
    c. the life of turtles.

8. Why do the penguins stand in turtles?
    a. They stand close together to keep warm.
    b. They want to be near their friends.
    c. They are not afraid when they stand together.

9. Which statement does the story lead you to believe?
    a. Emperor penguins cannot swim.
    b. Emperor penguins are small birds.
    c. Emperor penguins like to eat fish.

Strange Partners

When two people work together or help one another, they are partners. Sometimes two animals that are very different from one another can be partners, too.

The ratel (rā′təl) is a small unpleasant-looking animal that lives in Africa and Asia. Sometimes called the honey badger, the ratel is colored like a skunk.

The African ratel has a strange partner—a small bird known as the honey guide. Both the ratel and the honey guide love honey. They work together to get their favorite food.

With its sharp teeth and long claws, the ratel can break open beehives. Its tough hide protects the ratel from the stings of angry bees. The honey guide has the keen eyes needed to find a hive.

The ratel and honey guide travel together. The honey guide flies about until it spots a hive of wild bees. Then it calls out for its partner to follow. The honey guide leads the ratel to the hive by flying ahead of it. From time to time, the honey guide waits on a branch for the ratel to catch up.

When the two partners reach the hive, the honey guide waits patiently in a tree. The ratel rips open the hive. Then both animals get their share of honey. They have worked together, and now they enjoy their reward.

FIND THE ANSWERS

1. A ratel is sometimes called a
   - a. honey badger.
   - b. skunk.
   - c. honey guide.
   - d. small bird.

2. The word in paragraph 4 that means *strong and thick* is

   _____.

3. The words "small unpleasant-looking animal" in paragraph 2 describe

   the _____.

4. The story does not say so, but it makes you think that
   - a. the ratel does not have claws.
   - b. both the ratel and the honey guide eat bees.
   - c. ratels are larger than honey guides.

5. The job of the honey guide is to
   - a. find the beehive.
   - b. break open the hives.
   - c. chase away ratels.

6. The honey guide looks like a skunk.
   Yes   No   Does not say

7. On the whole, this story is about
   - a. partners that live in South America.
   - b. skunks and badgers that are partners.
   - c. two partners that like honey.

8. Why do the ratel and the honey guide work together?
   - a. They think it is fun to chase bees.
   - b. They enjoy playing together.
   - c. They both want to find honey.

9. Which statement does the story lead you to believe?
   - a. The honey guide does not see well.
   - b. The ratel is not a pretty animal.
   - c. The ratel and the honey guide look alike.

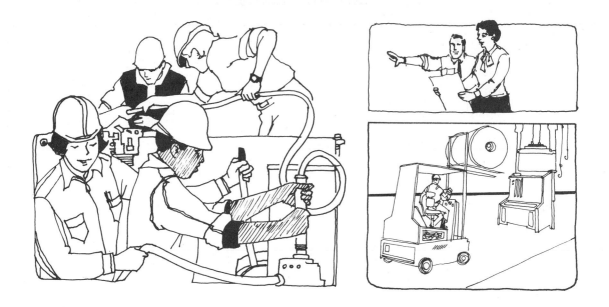

Who Runs a Factory?

A factory must have machines and the power to make them run. But who are the people who run a factory? A factory is run by a number of people with different skills who work together.

A factory must have engineers who can design new products and new machines for making them. A factory must have people to buy the needed parts and raw materials.

Factories must also have mechanics who understand machines and know how to keep them running. Other workers must check the finished product and make sure it is just as it should be. The factory must have salespeople who can sell its products.

Some workers in factories do not work with raw materials, machines, or products. However, their jobs are important, too. Some people hire the workers a factory needs. And there must be office workers to keep records, pay bills, and type letters.

In the past, a factory used many unskilled workers, or people who had no special skills. They did such jobs as lifting and carrying heavy loads. Now, machines do many of these jobs. More jobs are open to skilled workers who have special training. But it takes many people doing different jobs to run a factory.

FIND THE ANSWERS

1. A factory is run by
   a. many people.
   b. unskilled workers.
   c. engineers.
   d. mechanics.

2. The word in paragraph 3 that means *done* or *completed* is

   _____ .

3. The words "keep records, pay bills, and type letters" in paragraph 4

   describe _____ _____ .

4. The story does not say so, but it makes you think that
   a. factories do not need parts or raw materials.
   b. new factory products are designed by salespeople.
   c. many people in America work in factories.

5. The people who sell a factory's products are called
   a. engineers.
   b. salespeople.
   c. mechanics.

6. All factory workers run machines.
   Yes   No   Does not say

7. On the whole, this story is about
   a. the kinds of workers needed by factories.
   b. the kinds of power needed to run a factory.
   c. the kinds of products made in factories.

8. Why are there fewer jobs for unskilled workers today?
   a. Unskilled workers do not like to work in factories.
   b. Unskilled workers' jobs no longer have to be done.
   c. Machines are doing many of the unskilled workers' jobs.

9. Which statement does the story lead you to believe?
   a. A factory hires very few people.
   b. One person alone could not run a factory.
   c. All workers in a factory must know how to type.

Half Go Hungry

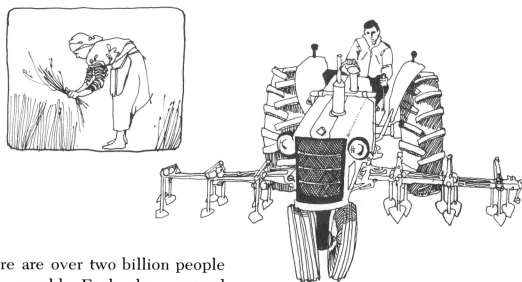

There are over two billion people in the world. Each day, around 324,000 babies are born, and the world's population grows larger.

At the present time, there is not enough food for everyone. More than half the world's population does not get enough of the right kinds of food to stay healthy. About 10,000 people in the world die of hunger every day.

Trying to feed the world's billions is a huge task. It is a job too large for some nations working alone. It is a job for many nations of the world working together. With the help of modern science, tools, and machinery, many countries can be helped to grow more food.

Over sixty countries have joined together to form the Food and Agriculture Organization of the United Nations. These nations work together to fight hunger.

The Food and Agriculture Organization searches for new and better ways to grow food. It helps fight animal and plant diseases. It sells seed to farmers at low cost. It works to turn deserts and waste lands into farming lands. It helps to improve the diets of the world's peoples. It sends teachers of agriculture into those countries that want help.

1. Every day, the world's population
   a. grows smaller.
   c. stays the same.
   b. does not change.
   d. grows larger.

2. The word in the first paragraph that means *all the people who live in a certain place* is _____.

3. The words "die of hunger every day" in paragraph 2 describe about 10,000 _____.

4. The story does not say so, but it makes you think that
   a. there is no way to fight hunger today.
   b. everybody gets enough food to eat.
   c. hungry people are being helped today.

5. Fighting hunger in the world is a job for
   a. many nations.
   b. one country.
   c. desert people.

6. Modern science can help countries grow more food.
   Yes   No   Does not say

7. On the whole, this story is about
   a. the number of babies being born.
   b. feeding hungry people everywhere.
   c. selling seed to farmers at low cost.

8. Why are the right foods important?
   a. They keep nations busy.
   b. They keep people modern.
   c. They keep people healthy.

9. Which statement does the story lead you to believe?
   a. Nations can work together to solve problems.
   b. Deserts should not be turned into farming land.
   c. Agriculture is the only subject that can be taught.

Defeating the Locusts

Each country tries to grow as much food as its land will allow. But humans are not the only ones who want to eat the food. Countries around the world have joined together in a daily battle with insect pests.

The locust is an insect pest that is found in many countries. It is a kind of grasshopper. From time to time, a group of locusts becomes so large that huge swarms leave the group. The swarms take wing and migrate, or fly from one place to another. They can migrate 2,000 miles.

Locusts eat crops, grass, and every plant they can find. They can destroy the food of millions. In Asia and Africa, clouds of desert locusts sometimes cover a country. The locust has been called a "stomach with wings."

Countries are now working together to defeat locusts. These insects often hatch in one country and migrate to another. Scientists study their lives and habits to find ways to fight them. People in countries around the world report on locust swarms. Since these insects are carried by winds, scientists know the paths the swarms will take.

Finally, planes are sent to the locust swarms. Sometimes the planes spread poisons over the locusts be-fore they can destroy crops in another country.

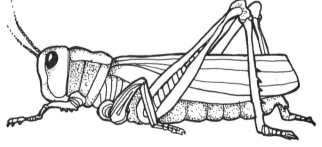

FIND THE ANSWERS

1. Locusts travel in
   a. flocks.
   b. swarms.
   c. clubs.
   d. groups.

2. The word in the first paragraph that means *nuisances* is

   _____ .

3. The words "carried by winds" in paragraph 4 refer to

   _____ .

4. The story does not say so, but it makes you think that
   a. locust swarms can never become very large.
   b. airplanes are sent to carry the locusts.
   c. locusts are a problem in many countries.

5. Locusts eat
   a. only in Asia and Africa.
   b. every plant they can find.
   c. insects that hatch food.

6. Locusts are of great help to humans.
   Yes   No   Does not say

7. On the whole, this story is about
   a. the way scientists study.
   b. poisons used for locusts.
   c. battling the locusts.

8. Why do scientists study the locusts?
   a. They want to find ways to fight them.
   b. They like to watch locusts destroy food.
   c. They want to travel in other countries.

9. Which statement does the story lead you to believe?
   a. Scientists may learn to control locusts.
   b. It is not good to spray locusts with poison.
   c. All locusts remain in one country in the world.

A Club for Everyone

On the little island of Bali (bä′lē), people did not like to work alone. The Balinese (bä′lə nēz′) thought a job was easier to do when there were many people to help. So that people could work together, the Balinese formed clubs.

Every Balinese village had many different kinds of clubs. Together, people in a club did the work they had to do or wanted to do. Farmers had clubs to water the rice fields. Small children had clubs to put on cricket fights or to fly kites. Young people joined clubs to give dances or to travel around the island.

Because the Balinese loved music, there were many orchestra clubs. Every orchestra had more people than it had instruments to play.

A person had only to announce the starting of a club. Soon there were many members for it. Since each club had more people than it needed for certain jobs, people took turns. People knew when it was their turn to do something. A person not doing a job had to pay a fine. The fines were small, but most people were happy to do their share of the work. People enjoyed working together.

FIND THE ANSWERS

1. On Bali, the farmers had clubs
   - a. to build barns.
   - b. to fight crickets.
   - c. to water rice fields.
   - d. to harvest crops.

2. The word in the first paragraph that means *not so hard* is

   _____.

3. The words "happy to do their share of work" in paragraph 4 describe

   most _____.

4. The story does not say so, but it makes you think that
   - a. Balinese people enjoy doing things alone.
   - b. not everyone belonged to the same club.
   - c. it was hard to get people to join the clubs.

5. People took turns
   - a. being happy on the job.
   - b. paying their fines.
   - c. doing certain jobs.

6. Even small children had clubs.

   Yes   No   Does not say

7. On the whole, this story is about
   - a. instruments that looked like clubs.
   - b. using clubs on Balinese people.
   - c. clubs on the island of Bali.

8. Why were there so many orchestra clubs?
   - a. The Balinese loved music.
   - b. The Balinese loved traveling.
   - c. They had a lot of instruments.

9. Which statement does the story lead you to believe?
   - a. The Balinese spend too much time flying kites.
   - b. People on Bali never get any work done.
   - c. The Balinese get along well together.

A Working Bee

The country of Panama is on the narrow strip of land that joins North America to South America. Its two major cities are both on the sea. The center of Panama has hills and mountains that are covered with thick forests.

The people who live in Panama's forests raise vegetable crops. They often have no close neighbors. Because of the many mountains and thick jungles, there are few roads or railroads. People travel on horseback or on foot.

Most farmers work their land much as the Indians did before Columbus' time. They work by hand, and their most important tool is a long, heavy knife called a machete (mə shet′ē).

A farm family may need help clearing the land, harvesting the crops, or building a barn or house. Then they invite their friends and neighbors to a working bee called a *junta* (hün′tə). *Junta* is from a Spanish word that means "to join."

At the *junta*, the men do the work and the women cook. The children do their part by taking food to the men.

When the work is finished, there is a feast for everyone. Some men play the guitars, violins, or drums that they have made by hand. The other people sing folk songs or dance to the pleasant music.

FIND THE ANSWERS

1. Panama is a country that joins North America with
   - a. South Australia.
   - b. the South Seas.
   - c. South Africa.
   - d. South America.

2. The word in paragraph 2 that means *wild, overgrown lands* is

   _____.

3. The words "dance to the pleasant music" in the last paragraph refer to

   other _____.

4. The story does not say so, but it makes you think that
   - a. Panama is not a very large country.
   - b. there are no major cities in Panama.
   - c. all of Panama is wide, open country.

5. A farm family may invite friends to
   - a. a working bee.
   - b. a spelling bee.
   - c. find some bees.

6. Most farmers use hand tools on their farms.
   Yes   No   Does not say

7. On the whole, this story is about
   - a. the hard work Indians do on farms.
   - b. life in the country of Panama.
   - c. a visit from Columbus to Panama.

8. Why do the people of Panama hold *juntas?*
   - a. They want the children to have fun.
   - b. The men want to play their guitars.
   - c. They wish to help the farmers.

9. Which statement does the story lead you to believe?
   - a. Everybody works at a *junta.*
   - b. Panama is filled with large cities.
   - c. There is too much singing at *juntas.*

Clubs for Boys and Girls

In our country, boys and girls often join clubs. The members of a club work together. They also learn certain skills and share good times.

Many boys in America belong to the Boy Scouts. Boy Scouts enjoy hiking and camping out together, and they learn many things. Scouts learn safety rules, first aid, and what to do in an emergency. Members have a chance to learn outdoor living. They learn to build fires, cook out in the open, and pitch tents.

Girl Scouts and Camp Fire Girls are clubs for girls. These two clubs give their members a chance to have fun and learn. The girls in a group take trips, have parties, and go hiking and camping together. The Camp Fire Girls earn honor beads for learning such skills as swimming and cooking. The Girl Scouts earn badges.

Both boys and girls are members of 4-H clubs. Children who live in either the city or the country may belong to 4-H. A project such as raising a pig or a calf can be carried on only by farm children. But city children can take part in gardening or cooking projects.

In all these clubs, members serve and work with their community. The boys and girls learn to be good and useful citizens.

1. Boy Scouts learn
   a. safety rules.
   b. to raise pigs.
   c. to trip in tents.
   d. to go to parties.

2. The word in paragraph 4 that means *plan* is _____.

3. The words "serve and work with their community" in the last paragraph

   describe club _____.

4. The story does not say so, but it makes you think that
   a. all Camp Fire Girls must raise a calf on a farm.
   b. Camp Fire Girls are proud when they earn beads.
   c. boys can join the Camp Fire Girls.

5. These clubs teach boys and girls how to
   a. live in big cities.
   b. enjoy all emergencies.
   c. be good, useful citizens.

6. The Boy Scouts learn about first aid.
   Yes   No   Does not say

7. On the whole, this story is about
   a. children who live in the city.
   b. some of the clubs for boys and girls.
   c. citizens who live in the community.

8. Why do boys and girls join clubs?
   a. They get beads and badges for joining.
   b. They learn how to work in a garden.
   c. They learn skills and share good times.

9. Which statement does the story lead you to believe?
   a. There are no clubs that take boys and girls together.
   b. The clubs teach boys and girls to get along with people.
   c. The only thing city children can learn to do is cook.

Children in a Chinese Commune

What would it be like to live and work in a Chinese commune? A commune is a group of people living and working together. The people share everything they have.

In communes in China today, children as well as older people work for the common good. Every one works, even the very young and the very old.

In China you would be only one of millions of children. Your grandmother might tell you about the days when she was a girl. At that time many people in China did not have enough food to eat. Many people did not have homes to live in. Things are different now. Everyone can belong to a commune where there is enough food.

Even children go to the town meetings. There the older people plan the work that needs to be done. No one is expected to quarrel about the work. At this meeting people learn what their work will be.

One child's job may be watching younger children. Another might be taught to repair machines. Everyone works hard so that the commune will be successful.

A commune has about 100 families who grow rice. Not everyone works in the fields. Some people go to the city to work and come back to the commune at night to sleep. They are glad to come home to their families.

In a Chinese commune, children have little time to be bored or unhappy. Like the older people, the children like to laugh and joke. People are happy that there is food to eat and work to do.

FIND THE ANSWERS

1. Older people in Chinese communes
   a. never work.   c. work every day.
   b. work with younger children.   d. retire at 65.

2. The word in paragraph 1 that means a *group of people living and working together* is _____.

3. The words "plan the work that needs to be done" in paragraph 4 describe the _____.

4. The story does not say so, but it makes you think that
   a. all grandmothers like to tell stories.
   b. there was always enough food in China long ago.
   c. life in China today is very different from long ago.

5. A child's job might be
   a. telling the commune what work to do.
   b. watching the younger children.
   c. walking to the city to work.

6. Even the very young and the very old work in a Chinese commune.
   Yes   No   Does not say

7. On the whole, this story is about
   a. people who go to the city to work.
   b. ways to fix things.
   c. people living in China today.

8. Why do Chinese children go to town meetings?
   a. They see shows.
   b. They play games.
   c. They hear the work being planned.

9. Which statement does the story lead you to believe?
   a. Chinese children smile a lot.
   b. Old people in China can do no work.
   c. Many people in China are happy to have food to eat and work to do.

A Peaceful Village

The pueblo (pweb'lō) Indians live in the American Southwest. They were farming the desert long before the first outsiders came to their land. Each Pueblo tribe lived together in adobe houses built high on a cliff. The houses were joined and made a Pueblo village look like an apartment house with many stories. A Pueblo village had about 2,000 people who lived and worked together.

The families in a Pueblo village were divided into clans. The clans worked together to keep the whole village peaceful and happy. Each clan chose members to go to a village council. The council settled the problems of the village. The clans also gave feasts and dances together.

The Pueblos believed it was important for people to work together and share. They thought that the rain gods would become angry if people could not work together in peace. Then there would be no rain.

If Pueblo children received any candy, they shared it with their brothers and sisters. If some people were grinding corn together, they worked at the same pace. No one tried to finish first. That would have been bad manners. If a family had poor luck farming, the others in the village gave the family food.

1. Pueblo tribes lived in adobe houses
   a. high on a cliff.
   b. in the valleys.
   c. near the sea.
   d. on the river.

2. The word in paragraph 4 that means *gave part of* is _____.

3. The words "gave feasts and dances together" in paragraph 2 describe

   the _____.

4. The story does not say so, but it makes you think that
   a. the Pueblos had too many angry gods.
   b. a village cannot be divided into clans.
   c. the village council had much power.

5. Pueblo families
   a. were all boys.
   b. shared many things.
   c. did no work.

6. Each clan had its own special name.
   Yes   No   Does not say

7. On the whole, this story is about
   a. rain gods who became angry at people.
   b. the number of stories in adobe houses.
   c. the Pueblo Indians of the Southwest.

8. Why was the council a good idea?
   a. It settled the problems of the village.
   b. The council knew how to make rain fall.
   c. It showed people how to grind corn.

9. Which statement does the story lead you to believe?
   a. People should learn to share what they have.
   b. The Pueblo Indians did not understand sharing.
   c. Pueblo children did not want to share candy.

Everyone Helps in the Congo

A village in the Congo rain forest in Africa is often built beside a river or lake. Two or three hundred people live in the village and farm the land around it. They also hunt and gather fruits and other foods from the jungle.

There is much work to be done in the village, and everyone does his or her share. Each person knows what he or she must do.

The men clear the land for farming and repair the houses. They make canoes from logs and weave plant fibers for mats and baskets. They get meat for the village by hunting and fishing.

The women plant, care for, and harvest the crops. They gather fruits, berries, and certain roots from the fields and jungle. They do the cooking.

The boys and girls have their jobs, too. They bring water from the river, and they feed the chickens. They help their mothers weed the gardens and care for younger brothers and sisters.

The people in the village help one another. The cleared land around the village is owned and cared for by all the villagers. They all share the crops. When people build a new house or repair their old one, their neighbors help. Everyone in the village must help repair the vine bridges that hang over streams filled with crocodiles.

1. In the Congo, crops are cared for by
   a. children.
   b. the whole family.
   c. women.
   d. brothers and sisters.

2. The word in paragraph 3 that means *fix* is _____.

3. The words "hang over streams filled with crocodiles" in the last paragraph describe the vine _____.

4. The story does not say so, but it makes you think that
   a. Congo villages are built in dry places.
   b. there is no water for farming the land.
   c. rivers or lakes are important to the people.

5. Cleared land is owned by
   a. the government.
   b. all the villagers.
   c. one family alone.

6. The people in the village share the work.
   Yes   No   Does not say

7. On the whole, this story is about
   a. the number of people in a village.
   b. feeding the chickens in a village.
   c. life in Congo rain forest villages.

8. Why do the people keep the vine bridges repaired?
   a. Vine bridges are pretty across streams.
   b. The streams are filled with crocodiles.
   c. It gives them something to do sometimes.

9. Which statement does the story lead you to believe?
   a. People in the village depend upon each other.
   b. People of the Congo do not care to help each other.
   c. People in Congo villages do not get along together.

Stories the Whole World Tells

What is a fairy story? What is a folk tale? These stories are told in every country in the world. People like to make up stories about their hopes and fears.

When people move to a new country, they take their fairy stories and folk tales from long ago. To their surprise they may hear stories in the new country that are like the old stories they brought with them.

Every country has special tales all its own. 2,000 years ago in northeast India, Guatama Buddha told many stories. Some stories told how people should think for themselves.

In many lands fables about animals are the favorite kind of story. A fable may teach lessons about how people act.

From Greece come the stories called Aesop's Fables. Aesop was a Greek slave who told stories about animals. From Africa come many more stories about animals. One writer named Joel Chandler Harris heard some of these animal stories. He retold them in a book called *Uncle Remus: His Songs and His Sayings.* From Scotland come tales of mermaids and mermen from under the sea. From Ireland come stories about little green leprechauns.

People believe these stories help them to understand their problems. But most of all, stories entertain people. Whether the ending is sad or glad, people will always enjoy telling stories to each other.

FIND THE ANSWERS

1. Fairy stories and folk tales
   a. are told in every country in the world.   c. are easy to forget.
   b. are told only in India.   d. are no longer told.

2. The word in paragraph 1 that means *a story* is _____.

3. The words "may teach lessons about how people act" in paragraph 4

   refer to a _____.

4. The story does not say so, but it makes you think that
   a. animals would like to write stories about people.
   b. people dislike stories about other people.
   c. some of the best folk stories are about animals.

5. Stories from Scotland tell about
   a. little green leprechauns.
   b. mermaids and mermen from under the sea.
   c. people who think for themselves.

6. People believe stories help them to understand their problems.
   Yes   No   Does not say

7. On the whole, this story is about
   a. stories being alike in countries all over the world.
   b. animals following people from country to country.
   c. the way Aesop wrote African stories.

8. Why do people find old fairy stories in new countries?
   a. They wish they were back in their old country.
   b. They find that people and their stories are much the same.
   c. They think all stories are alike.

9. Which statement does the story lead you to believe?
   a. Joel Chandler Harris could not make up his own stories.
   b. Leprechauns can be any color they choose.
   c. New stories and folk tales will always be told.

Up the Highest Mountain

Centuries ago, mountains were thought to be the home of evil spirits. It was not until 200 years ago that humans began to climb the highest peaks.

At first they climbed alone or with one or two friends. However, as people climbed higher and more dangerous mountains, a team who could work together became very important.

Climbing a giant mountain takes weeks and even months. The climbers must set up many camps as they climb upward. They must also take along tons of supplies. They need food, warm clothes, and tanks of oxygen.

In 1953, a team of climbers from England set out to conquer Mt. Everest. They had to plan carefully. As yet, no one had been able to reach the top.

Mt. Everest is far from highways and railroads. People from the neighboring country of Nepal (nə pôl′) joined the mountain-climbing party. They would help carry the needed supplies through the mountains. Each person would carry a very heavy pack. The people of Nepal had carried goods across those mountains for centuries. A helper who took packs to the highest camps earned the name "tiger."

Together, the helpers and climbers worked their way up Everest. At last, two climbers went ahead. They pushed on to the top. The highest mountain in the world had been conquered.

1. People who climb mountains must take
   a. tanks of oxygen.   c. giants with them.
   b. evil spirits along.   d. their neighbors.

2. The word in the first paragraph that means *bad* or *harmful* is

   _____.

3. The words "they need food" in paragraph 3 refer to the

   _____.

4. The story does not say so, but it makes you think that
   a. danger does not keep people from climbing mountains.
   b. anyone can climb high mountains in England.
   c. helpers who carry packs might turn into tigers.

5. Climbers who conquered Mount Everest were from
   a. Germany.
   b. Russia.
   c. England.

6. It takes weeks or months to climb a giant mountain.
   Yes   No   Does not say

7. On the whole, this story is about
   a. climbing Mount Everest.
   b. people carrying goods.
   c. tigers in mountains.

8. Why were people once afraid to climb mountains?
   a. They thought it was too lonely in the mountains.
   b. They thought mountains were the home of evil spirits.
   c. They thought the mountains were filled with tigers.

9. Which statement does the story lead you to believe?
   a. It takes teamwork to conquer a dangerous mountain.
   b. Too many people are climbing mountains in Nepal.
   c. It is not necessary for climbers to take supplies.

On the Floor of the Sea

If people are to make full use of the sea, they must be able to live and work under water. In the fall of 1965, an undersea house called Conshelf Three was lowered to the sea floor. Inside were six divers. It was their job to prove that people can live and work 328 feet below the ocean's surface.

A year of planning, testing, training, and building had gone into this project. It depended on many people working together.

The six divers down below worked as a team. They were alone in their world below the sea. In their undersea house they ate and slept. Wearing special suits, they left their house through a hatch. They could not rise to the surface because the sudden change in water pressure might kill them.

Outside their house the ocean was black as night and very cold. The divers used their own lighting to see. They studied the ocean floor around them and took pictures. They did hard tasks to prove that people can work beneath the ocean.

Up above, people were working as a team to keep the divers safe. They watched the divers below on TV. They checked instruments to make sure all was going well.

After three weeks, Conshelf Three was brought back to the surface. Divers working together had given us new information about the sea.

1. The six divers ate and slept
   a. on the surface.
   b. on a large shelf.
   c. in their undersea house.
   d. in their own houses.

2. The word in the first paragraph that means *let down* is

   _____ .

3. The words "black as night and very cold" in paragraph 4 describe the

   _____ .

4. The story does not say so, but it makes you think that
   a. no one has ever seen the bottom of the sea.
   b. people should live in undersea houses.
   c. there is no light deep in the ocean.

5. Conshelf Three was brought back to the surface
   a. after three weeks.
   b. within ten minutes.
   c. after five months.

6. The divers could rise to the surface from their house.
   Yes   No   Does not say

7. On the whole, this story is about
   a. the color of the ocean.
   b. the people who kept the divers safe.
   c. learning to work beneath the ocean.

8. Why couldn't the divers rise to the surface?
   a. The sudden changes in water pressure would kill them.
   b. The divers could not swim that far in their suits.
   c. They were not able to see where they were going.

9. Which statement does the story lead you to believe?
   a. People do not have to wear special suits in the sea.
   b. Conshelf Three is still at the bottom of the sea.
   c. People may make full use of the sea someday.

Letters around the World

Every day millions of letters go from one country to another. Letters mailed in Italy are received in Japan. Letters mailed in Canada are received in Africa. On the letters are many different kinds of stamps, bought in different countries.

The Universal Postal Union helps each letter get to the right place as quickly as possible. It sets up rules about the size and weight of letters, postcards, and small packages. It has rules that all countries must follow about international postal rates.

One hundred years ago, international mail did not move so smoothly. One country did not always accept another country's letters. Letters from some countries were too large to fit into the mailboxes of other countries. Letters traveled by many different routes. Some were lost along the way.

Sometimes the person who sent the letter could pay only part of the postage. The person receiving the letter had to pay the rest.

The United States was the first to suggest that all countries work together to settle the questions of international mail. In 1874, people from twenty-two countries met in Switzerland to form the Universal Postal Union. Today, more than 120 nations belong to the union. From its office in Switzerland, the union helps the mail move safely and quickly around the world.

FIND THE ANSWERS

1. The Universal Postal Union
   a. buys stamps.
   b. makes rules.
   c. moves mailboxes.
   d. loses letters.

2. The word in paragraph 5 that means *to advise* is _____.

3. The words "too large to fit into the mailboxes" in paragraph 3 describe the _____.

4. The story does not say so, but it makes you think that
   a. mail is important to all countries.
   b. not enough letters are sent to Japan.
   c. all stamps look exactly the same.

5. People from twenty-two countries met in
   a. South Africa.
   b. Switzerland.
   c. Scandinavia.

6. Different countries sell different kinds of stamps.
   Yes   No   Does not say

7. On the whole, this story is about
   a. small packages.
   b. letters in Italy.
   c. international mail.

8. Why was the Universal Postal Union formed?
   a. It was formed to help move mail quickly around the world.
   b. It was formed to give many people a chance to work.
   c. It was formed to help people meet in Switzerland.

9. Which statement does the story lead you to believe?
   a. Countries around the world need each other's help.
   b. Most people do not put enough postage on letters.
   c. It is not possible for letters to get lost on the way.

Saving the Seals

Who owns the sea? The ships of all countries sail the open seas. Not long ago, all countries could fish and hunt in the ocean as they pleased. Now, the countries using the sea must work together to protect the sea's animal life.

In 1870, there were millions of valuable fur seals in the Bering Sea. Ships came from all parts of the world to kill them. People wanted the animals' fur and the oil from their bodies. By 1910, only about 130,000 seals were left. Even the hunters knew that something had to be done or the seals would disappear.

Four countries owned land near the seals' northern home. In 1911, these countries began plans to control seal hunting. The governments of Japan, Russia, Canada, and the United States agreed to kill no more seals in the open seas. They wanted to protect seals on the rocky islands where the animals rested and had their young. Only male seals that did not have mates could be killed. Money earned from the skins and oil of these seals was to be divided among the four governments.

Today, large herds of seals swim in the Bering Sea again. By working together, four countries saved the seals in the sea they share.

FIND THE ANSWERS

1. Today, large herds of seals swim in the
   - a. South Seas.
   - b. Arabian Sea.
   - c. Bering Sea.
   - d. Dead Sea.

2. The word in paragraph 2 that means *to be gone forever* or *to be lost* is

   _____.

3. The words "rested and had their young" in paragraph 3 refer to the

   _____.

4. The story does not say so, but it makes you think that
   - a. hunters used seal oil on their bodies.
   - b. seals have little value for hunters.
   - c. all the seals might have been killed.

5. Money earned from seals was divided among
   - a. the large herds.
   - b. too many countries.
   - c. four governments.

6. Fourteen countries agreed to protect the seals.
   Yes   No   Does not say

7. On the whole, this story is about
   - a. Russia and Canada.
   - b. protecting seals.
   - c. the rocky islands.

8. Why were the seals hunted?
   - a. People wanted to eat seal meat.
   - b. Their fur and oil were valuable.
   - c. The seals were eating all the fish.

9. Which statement does the story lead you to believe?
   - a. Seals will have to leave the Bering Sea.
   - b. It is important to protect sea animals.
   - c. Only one country should hunt seals.

Checking on the Weather

Winds do not stop when they come to a boundary line. They swing around the world, causing changes in the weather.

Cold air can move south from the far North and harm crops and cattle in the American Southwest. Winds from the Sahara Desert can carry dust all the way across a sea to Italy. Winds from Mexico can sweep into the United States.

Since many countries share weather, they also share weather reports. Since 1853, there has been a world organization that gathers weather information. It passes this information on to any country that needs it.

Since 1951, this work has been done by the World Meteorological (mē′tē ər ə loj′ə kl) Organization in Switzerland. This office has 8,000 weather stations in all parts of the world. The stations report to the office each day. Thousands of ships and airplanes also send reports about the weather at sea and in the air. Certain stations watch for hurricanes and send out warnings when such storms come near.

Weather bureaus get information they need from the world organization. They can then tell farmers when to expect frost. They can tell ships when to change their courses. They can tell airplane pilots where storms are so they can fly around them.

Weather crosses boundaries, and so do weather reports.

FIND THE ANSWERS

1. Weather bureaus get information they need from
   a. the Sahara Desert. c. the American Southwest.
   b. the United States. d. a world organization.

2. The word in the first paragraph that means *border* is _____.

3. The words "carry dust all the way across a sea" in paragraph 2 describe the _____.

4. The story does not say so, but it makes you think that winds
   a. must stop at the boundary.
   b. can cause much damage.
   c. in Mexico come from Italy.

5. Warnings are sent out by
   a. people in Mexico.
   b. ships and airplanes.
   c. airplane pilots.

6. Countries get their weather information from farmers.
   Yes   No   Does not say

7. On the whole, this story is about
   a. cattle in the Southwest.
   b. sharing weather reports.
   c. ships changing courses.

8. Why is it a good idea to have a world organization?
   a. It can make the weather change for the farmers.
   b. It helps different countries share their storms.
   c. It can give weather information to all countries.

9. Which statement does the story lead you to believe?
   a. Weather reports warn only farmers.
   b. Weather reports help many people.
   c. Weather reports cause many storms.

The Fort That Became a Museum

From early times, humans have been interested in art. People have often worked together to collect and save the world's art treasures.

Fine art treasures from many countries are kept in an art museum called the Louvre (lü′vrə) in Paris, France. The works of art have been collected by the people of France over many centuries.

The Louvre has not always been a museum. The first building was a fort. In 1190, it was a royal castle with high walls and a round tower. It had a moat to keep out enemies.

Over the years, the number of buildings around the castle grew. By 1350, the castle was no longer needed as a fort. The Louvre became a palace home for French kings and queens.

During times of peace, new treasures were brought in. During days of war, many treasures were stolen, and the buildings were damaged.

When Francis I became King of France in 1515, he brought in artists from many countries. One of the artists was Leonardo da Vinci (lā ə när′dō də vin′chē) from Italy. Da Vinci's "Mona Lisa" is the best-known painting in the museum today.

In 1793, the Louvre became a public museum, just as it is now. It is a place where art treasures have been saved for everyone to enjoy.

FIND THE ANSWERS

1. The Louvre was once
   a. a large moat.
   b. a palace home.
   c. an artist's house.
   d. an English castle.

2. The word in the first paragraph that means *to bring together* is

   _____ .

3. The words "with high walls and a round tower" in paragraph 3 describe

   a royal _____ .

4. The story does not say so, but it makes you think that
   a. the Louvre is only for artists.
   b. many people visit the Louvre.
   c. da Vinci lives in the Louvre.

5. King Francis I of France brought in artists from
   a. an old fort.
   b. France only.
   c. many countries.

6. The Louvre has been used in several different ways.
   Yes   No   Does not say

7. On the whole, this story is about
   a. an art museum called the Louvre.
   b. an artist named Leonardo da Vinci.
   c. kings and queens of France.

8. Why is it good for great art to be kept in public museums?
   a. It helps people remember who the kings and queens are.
   b. It keeps people out of the royal palaces.
   c. It gives everyone a chance to enjoy good art.

9. Which statement does the story lead you to believe?
   a. Great art should be shared with all the people.
   b. Old forts always make the best museums.
   c. It is not possible for treasures to be stolen.

The Flood at Florence

The city of Florence, Italy, has been a center of art and learning since the Middle Ages. The scientist Galileo once walked its streets and studied the heavens through his new telescope. Authors and artists worked there. Its churches and museums hold valuable art pieces. Its library is the largest in Italy.

In November 1966, the treasures of Florence were almost destroyed. Nineteen inches of rain came down in two days. The rising Arno River roared over its banks and rushed through the streets. Over 500,000 tons of mud swept into the city.

There was not time to move books and paintings. Works of art were coated with mud and oil. Walls and statues were in danger of crumbling. News of the flood went out to the world.

As the water went down, an army of helpers moved into Florence. Some of them were trained workers who knew how to treat the damaged pictures and books. Most of them were young people from more than a dozen countries. Dressed in blue work clothes, they went to work with brooms and shovels. They carried books and paintings to safe places. They worked hour after hour without pay.

People around the world had often gone to Florence to look at its treasures. When Florence needed help, they came to work.

1. In November 1966, the treasures of Florence were
   a. taken to Galileo.   c. almost destroyed.
   b. in a library.   d. given away.

2. The word in paragraph 4 that means *harmed* is _____.

3. The words "roared over its banks and rushed through the streets" in

   paragraph 2 refer to the rising _____ _____.

4. The story does not say so, but it makes you think that
   a. the art treasures of Florence were valued everywhere.
   b. there is no way to save art treasures in Florence.
   c. the art treasures of Florence belonged to Galileo.

5. Works of art were
   a. waxed and polished with oil.
   b. coated with mud and oil.
   c. kept safe with oil and water.

6. All Florence's art treasures were lost in the flood.
   Yes   No   Does not say

7. On the whole, this story is about
   a. saving the art treasures of Florence.
   b. how much mud swept into the city.
   c. the way walls and statues can crumble.

8. Why didn't the people of Florence move the paintings?
   a. They were in the bank.
   b. They had no army.
   c. There was no time.

9. Which statement does the story lead you to believe?
   a. People must dress in blue work clothes to help.
   b. Many people are helpful in times of trouble.
   c. No one outside Florence knew about the flood.

Saving the Treasures

Fire! There were flames shooting into the night sky from beautiful St. Paul's Cathedral in Antwerp (ant′wərp), Belgium. For 400 years the Belgian people had loved the cathedral and the fine paintings on its walls. The church held paintings by famous artists such as Van Dyck and Rubens. Now it looked as if the cathedral and everything in it would burn.

Near the church were restaurants and dance halls. Many young people and art students were dancing and having a good time. When they saw the fire, they rushed to the church. They began to carry out pictures. They were at work before either the fire engines or the police arrived.

Even though the building was burning, the youths worked on. They jumped past burning wood beams that fell around them. They carried pictures, wood carvings, and small statues through the smoke.

When the fire was out, the building was badly damaged. But more than 10 million dollars' worth of paintings were safe. Their value in money meant little to the students. Money could not bring back a single famous painting. By risking their lives, the young men and women had saved the work of great artists for everyone to enjoy.

1. Many fine paintings were in the Antwerp
    a. museum.
    c. restaurants.
    b. cathedral.
    d. dance halls.

2. The word in the first paragraph that means *well known* is

    _____.

3. The words "badly damaged" in the last paragraph describe the

    _____.

4. The story does not say so, but it makes you think that
    a. all famous paintings are not in museums.
    b. paintings in cathedrals catch on fire.
    c. paintings should be kept in dance halls.

5. The young people risked their lives to
    a. eat in restaurants near a church.
    b. keep the fire engines away.
    c. save the work of great artists.

6. The cathedral in Antwerp was badly damaged.
    Yes   No   Does not say

7. On the whole, this story is about
    a. flames shooting into the night.
    b. fire engines rushing in a city.
    c. the brave young people of Antwerp.

8. Why did the young people care little about the money value of the paintings?
    a. The young people did not know the value of money.
    b. Money could not bring back any of the paintings.
    c. The young people had more than enough money already.

9. Which statement does the story lead you to believe?
    a. Cathedrals can only be found in Antwerp, Belgium.
    b. The young people treasured the great paintings.
    c. Young people in Antwerp dance in their churches.

The Weaving Contest
(A Greek Folktale)

Long ago in a small village in Greece, there lived a girl named Arachne (ə rak'nē) who liked to spin and weave. So beautiful was her weaving that she became famous throughout the land.

People came from near and far to watch Arachne weave. Everyone had words of praise for her. Some said, "To watch Arachne weave is a wonderful sight." Others said, "Arachne's fingers must have magic in them!"

Arachne was proud of her beautiful weaving. As time went on, she grew prouder still. She would often boast, "No one else has such skill!" Then she would smile proudly and add, "I am the best weaver in all the land."

One day, a large crowd gathered around Arachne as she sat at her loom. Someone asked her, "Who taught you how to weave so well? Was it the Goddess Athena herself?"

Now Athena looked after women's skills. Through her blessing alone could any woman become a good weaver.

Arachne looked down at her wonderful work. "No," she said, "the Goddess Athena did not teach me how to weave. She is a good weaver, but I am even better."

The people who watched drew back in surprise. No woman ever said she was better than a goddess.

While Arachne boasted, the Goddess Athena listened. She was a powerful and important goddess. When she heard what Arachne said, she was not pleased. She said to herself, "No girl should boast as much as this one. How can this girl say that she weaves better than a goddess? I weave for the gods!"

The Goddess Athena disguised herself as an old woman and went to Arachne. She told Arachne patiently, "You may say that you weave better than other people. But it is wrong to say you weave better than a goddess. You must ask the Goddess Athena to forgive you. Otherwise, something terrible will happen to you."

Arachne did not know that the old woman was the Goddess Athena in disguise. She acted as proud as ever, and she laughed at the old woman's warning.

Arachne threw back her head. "Silly old woman! I will say what I like. I am not afraid of Athena. Besides, my weaving is better than hers. Even the forest spirits leave their woodland homes to look at my wonderful work."

Athena, still in her old woman's disguise, was beginning to grow cross. She asked Arachne, "What would you do if Athena could hear you? Would you not be afraid of her anger? Would you not be sorry you had boasted?"

Arachne only boasted more. She said, "I wish Athena *were* here! I would dare her to have a weaving contest with me. Then all the world would know I weave better than a goddess."

At that, Athena became quite angry. She threw off her disguise and shouted, "Here I am! Let the contest begin!"

Everyone was frightened to see the Goddess Athena standing there. They all bowed down low to her. Arachne turned pale, but she would not say she was sorry.

The contest started. Athena and Arachne sat down at their looms and began to weave. Everyone watched quietly. Never had they seen such weaving!

When the contest was over, Athena looked at Arachne's work. The weaving was both perfect and beautiful. But Arachne's weaving showed pictures that made fun of the gods and goddesses. She showed them as ugly animals and birds.

Athena was more angry than ever. She cried out, "No one can make fun of a goddess! For punishment, you should die."

But Athena looked once more at

Arachne's beautiful work. It was as perfect as her own. So she said, "Because you are such a fine weaver, you shall not die. Instead, you shall spin and weave forever."

With those words, Athena sprinkled Arachne with a magic powder. Arachne grew smaller and smaller. At last she turned into a spider.

In any garden, you can see Arachne yet, spinning her silver thread and weaving her wonderful webs.

664 words

Fill in your record chart after each test. Beside the page numbers, put a one for each correct question. Put zero in the box of each question you missed. At the far right, put your total. Nine is a perfect score for each test.

When you finish all the tests in a concept, total your scores by question. The highest possible score for each question in one concept is the number of stories.

When you have taken several tests, check to see which questions you get right each time. Which ones are you missing? Find the places where you need help. For example, if you are missing Question 3 often, ask for help in learning to use directing words.

As you begin each concept, copy the chart onto lined paper. Down the left side are the test page numbers. Across the top are the question numbers and the kinds of questions. For example, each Question 1 in this book asks you to recall a fact. Your scores for each question show how well you are learning each skill.

Your Reading Scores   Concept I

Page 15 Question	1 fact	2 vocabulary	3 modification	4 inference	5 fact	6 confirming content	7 main idea	8 cause and effect	9 inference	Total for Page
17										
19										
21										
23										
25										
27										
29										
31										
33										
35										
37										
39										
41										
43										
45										
47										
49										
Totals by question										

Your Reading Scores   Concept III

Question / Page	1 fact	2 vocabulary	3 modification	4 inference	5 fact	6 confirming content	7 main idea	8 cause and effect	9 inference	Total for Page
113										
115										
117										
119										
121										
123										
125										
127										
129										
131										
133										
135										
137										
139										
141										
143										
145										
147										
149										
151										
153										
155										
157										
159										
161										
163										
165										
Totals by question										

Your Reading Scores   Concept II

Question / Page	1 fact	2 vocabulary	3 modification	4 inference	5 fact	6 confirming content	7 main idea	8 cause and effect	9 inference	Total for Page
55										
57										
59										
61										
63										
65										
67										
69										
71										
73										
75										
77										
79										
81										
83										
85										
87										
89										
91										
93										
95										
97										
99										
101										
103										
105										
107										
Totals by question										

WORDS YOU WILL NEED

These are words and names that are hard to read. Learn how to say each word. Find the word in the story. Learn the meaning. Use the word in a sentence of your own. The words are only listed once. You will need the words you learned to read the stories that follow.

5 6 7 8 9 10 VHVH 86 85 84 83 82 81